Cooperative Games and Sports

Joyful Activities for Everyone

Second Edition

Terry Orlick, PhD

Human Kinetics

Library of Congress Cataloging-in-Publication Data

Orlick, Terry.

Cooperative games and sports : joyful activities for everyone / Terry Orlick.-- 2nd ed.

p. cm.

ISBN-10: 0-7360-5797-8 (soft cover)

ISBN-13: 978-0-7360-5797-4

1. Games. 2. Sports. 3. Cooperation. 4. Family recreation. I. Title.

GV1201.O7 2006

793--dc22

2005037032

ISBN-10: 0-7360-5797-8

ISBN-13: 978-0-7360-5797-4

This book is a revised edition of *The Cooperative Sports & Games Book: Challenge Without Competition*, published in 1978 by Pantheon Books.

The Web addresses cited in this text were current as of January 2006, unless otherwise noted.

Acquisitions Editor: Scott Wikgren; **Managing Editor:** Jacqueline Eaton Blakley; **Assistant Editor:** Kathleen Bernard; **Copyeditor:** Patricia MacDonald; **Proofreader:** Ann M. Augspurger; **Permission Manager:** Dalene Reeder; **Graphic Designer:** Fred Starbird; **Graphic Artist:** Kathleen Boudreau-Fuoss; **Photo Manager:** Sarah Ritz; **Cover Designer:** Keith Blomberg; **Photographer (covers):** Wim Kok; **Photographer (interior):** Wim Kok: pages 1, 4, 7, 9, 10, 16, 17, 19, 21, 25, 27, 28, 30, 33, 34, 38, 39, 40, 44, 50, 55, 56, 57, 58, 59, 70, 118, 136, 138, 147, 152, Sarah Ritz: pages 73, 75, 76, 77, 79, 81, 82, 85, 87, 93, 94, 96, 99, 101, 103, 104, Terry Orlick: pages 42, 109, 112, 125, 126, 133, Bellsa Orlick: page 115, and Human Kinetics: page 119; **Printer:** Versa Press

We thank the YMCA in Champaign, IL, for assistance in providing the location for the photo shoot for this book.

Human Kinetics books are available at special discounts for bulk purchase. Special editions or book excerpts can also be created to specification. For details, contact the Special Sales Manager at Human Kinetics.

Printed in the United States of America 10 9 8 7 6 5 4 3 2 1

Human Kinetics
Web site: www.HumanKinetics.com

United States: Human Kinetics
P.O. Box 5076
Champaign, IL 61825-5076
800-747-4457
e-mail: humank@hkusa.com

Canada: Human Kinetics
475 Devonshire Road Unit 100
Windsor, ON N8Y 2L5
800-465-7301 (in Canada only)
e-mail: orders@hkcanada.com

Europe: Human Kinetics
107 Bradford Road, Stanningley
Leeds LS28 6AT, United Kingdom
+44 (0) 113 255 5665
e-mail: hk@hkeurope.com

Australia: Human Kinetics
57A Price Avenue, Lower Mitcham
South Australia 5062
08 8277 1555
e-mail: liaw@hkaustralia.com

New Zealand: Human Kinetics
Division of Sports Distributors NZ Ltd.
P.O. Box 300 226 Albany
North Shore City, Auckland
0064 9 448 1207
e-mail: info@humankinetics.co.nz

Contents

Acknowledgments iv

Activity Finder v

CHAPTER 1 Who Needs Cooperative Games? 1

CHAPTER 2 Games for Children Ages 3 Through 7 9

CHAPTER 3 Games for Children Ages 8 Through 12 73

CHAPTER 4 Games for Preschoolers 109

CHAPTER 5 Remaking Adult Games 118

CHAPTER 6 Cooperative Games From Other Cultures 125

CHAPTER 7 Creating Your Own Games and Evaluating Your Success 136

CHAPTER 8 A New Beginning: Turning Ideas Into Positive Action 152

Appendix: Cooperative Play Days 157

Resources 160

About the Author 163

This book is dedicated to the millions of wonderful people in our world who nurture a sense of harmony, joy, and caring in our children, our games, and our lives. People like you give our children and our world some legitimate hope for the future.

What Every Child Wants
As a child,
I want to feel excited—every day.
I want to feel fully alive.
I want to feel fully accepted.
I want to feel fully supported.
I want to feel important and valued.
I want to experience this day, and every day, as a gift worth living.

Let us help our children feel this way every day.

What Every Adult Wants
As an adult,
I want to feel excited about something—every day.
I want to feel fully alive.
I want to feel fully accepted.
I want to feel fully supported.
I want to feel important and valued.
I want to experience this day, and every day, as a gift worth living.

Let us help ourselves and our loved ones feel this way every day.

Acknowledgments

Creating cooperative games and writing a book on cooperative games are a collaborative venture—I couldn't have done it all on my own. There are many people to whom I am grateful for enhancing the quality of this new edition of *Cooperative Games and Sports.*

Thanks to my youngest daughters and greatest teachers, Jewelia and Skye. Thanks to my wife, Bellsa, for the gift of time—without her support I would not have been able to complete this second edition. Thanks to the wonderful children, teachers, principal, and parents at Chelsea Elementary School and Chelsea Cooperative Nursery School: Michelle McMahon and Maureen Fehr (nursery school teachers), Janet Busby (kindergarten teacher), and Katie Gray (Meech Lake Co-op Games Coordinator). Finally, thanks to photographer Wim Kok and my teammates at Human Kinetics: Rainer Martens, Scott Wikgren, Jackie Blakley, and Kathleen Bernard.

Thank you all for your cooperation, caring, and commitment to excellence in what you do.

Simple Joys,

Terry Orlick

Activity Finder

Because this book contains more than 150 activities, you might find it challenging to remember where each one is located! This simple table will help you find activities by name. They are listed in alphabetical order; simply find the name of the activity and locate its page number in the corresponding row.

In addition, this finder shows you at a glance which activities require equipment. (Y means equipment is called for; N means no equipment is needed; O means equipment is optional.) Keep in mind that "equipment" often refers to simple, readily available objects, not necessarily specialized gear.

Other relevant categories included in this finder are the age range that the games work best with, the approximate number of players per group or team ("any" means as many children as can fit in the play space and still have room to move around freely), the general activity level involved in games (VA signifies a very active game, A means active, and Q stands for quiet), and whether it may be played indoors (I), outdoors (O), or both (B).

Activity name	Equipment	Ages	Number of players	Activity level	Indoors/ outdoors	Page(s)
Aboriginal Winning Marbles	Y	6 and up	Any	Q	B	127
Action	Y	8-12	Any	VA	B	141-142
Airplane Carry	N	10 and up	Any	VA	B	133-134
All on One Side	Y	7 and up	4-6 per team	A	B	102
Aura	N	6 and up	Any	Q	B	91
Balancing Bridges	Y	5 and up	Any	A	B	62
Balloon Bucket (Collective Hoops)	Y	7 and up	Any	A	B	103-104
Balloon Keep-Up	Y	3 and up	Any	A	B	15-16

(continued)

Activity name	Equipment	Ages	Number of players	Activity level	Indoors/ outdoors	Page(s)
Barnyard	N	3 and up	Any	A	B	25-26
Baseball Tennis	Y	7 and up	6-9 per team	A	B	144
Basket-Football	Y	9 and up	5-8 per team	A	B	145
Beach-Ball Balance	Y	3-10	Any	Q	B	17-18
Beat the Clock	Y	7-10	6-8 per group	A	B	142
Big Snake	N	3-8	10-14 per group	A	B	30
Big Turnip	N	3-6	8-10 per group	Q	B	135
Big Turtle	Y	3-8	8-10	A	B	28-29
Blanket Toss	Y	8 and up	Any	A	B	132
Blanketball	Y	9 and up	7-9 per team	A	B	100-101
Box Ball	Y	8 and up	Any	A	B	87-88
Bull's Eye	N	3 and up	Any	A	B	72
Bump and Scoot	Y	8 and up	7-10 per side	A	B	98-99
Bump and Team Scoot	Y	8 and up	7-10 per side	VA	B	99-100
Candle Carry	Y	10 and up	Any	Q	B	92
Carry On	Y	8 and up	Any	A	B	89
Caterpillar Over the Mountain	Y	3-8	6-12 per group	A	B	27-28
Changing Channels	Y	5 and up	Any	Q	B	108
Cherry Bowl	Y	8 and up	Any	Q	O	83
Children Teaching Children	N	3 and up	3 per team	A	B	117
Circle of Friends	N	8 and up	6-9 per group	A	B	80-81

Activity name	Equipment	Ages	Number of players	Activity level	Indoors/ outdoors	Page(s)
Collective Orbit	Y	9 and up	Any	A	B	104-105
Collective Pin	Y	7 and up	5-8 per team	Q	B	127
Collective Rounders	Y	8 and up	8-10 per team	A	B	105-106
Collective-Score Blanketball	Y	9 and up	7-9 per side	A	B	101-102
Collective-Score Monsterball	Y	11and up	8-10 per side	A	B	102-103
Collective-Score Towel Ball	Y	11and up	8-10 per side	A	B	144
Cooperative Balloons Through Hoops	Y	4 and up	Any	A	B	16-17
Cooperative Cycling	N	4 and up	Any	A	B	58-59
Cooperative Hide and Seek	N	3 and up	Any	A	B	116
Cooperative Musical Chairs	Y	4-8	8-12	A	B	21-23
Cooperative Musical Hugs	Y	3 and up	Any	VA	B	44
Cooperative Pin the Tail on the Donkey	Y	3 and up	6-7 per group	Q	B	116
Cooperative Sit-Ups	Y	3 and up	Any	A	B	75
Cooperative Trains	N	4-9	8-24 per group	VA	B	41-42
Crossover Dodgeball	Y	7 and up	Any	A	B	79-80
Dog Sledge	Y	8 and up	Any	VA	B	134
Double Bubble	N	3-7	Any	A	B	33-34
Double Partner Tube Rebounding	Y	6 and up	Any	A	B	76
Draw and Sing a Song	Y	8 and up	Any	Q	B	92
Eco-Ball	N	3 and up	Any	A	B	72

(continued)

Activity name	Equipment	Ages	Number of players	Activity level	Indoors/ outdoors	Page(s)
Eskimo Winning Marbles	Y	6 and up	Any	Q	B	132
Esti-Time	N	8 and up	Any	A	B	84-85
Evanena (Walking Down the Pole)	N	8 and up	Any	A	B	128
Exactly the Same Time	N	3 and up	Any	Q/A	B	53-54
Family of Elephants	O	3-7	Any	A	B	31
Find Your Animal	Y	7-10	Any	Q	B	142
Fish Gobbler	N	3-9	20-30 per group	VA	B	40-41
Freeing Your Friends	Y	3-9	Any	A	B	24-25
Frozen Tag	N	5 and up	Any	A	B	78-79
Fruit Cocktail	Y	6 and up	Any	A	B	84
Gesture Name Game	N	3 and up	8-12 per group	A	B	11-12
Giant People and Animals	N	4-8	6-12 per group	A	B	31-32
Grasshopper in the Blanket	Y	3 and up	7-12 per group	A	B	38-39
Gym Hattette	Y	8 and up	6 per team	A	B	143
Helping Grow the Flowers	Y	3-6	6 per group	A	B	134-135
Here We Come Walking	N	3-7	12-20	A	B	64-65
Highlight Charades	N	3 and up	5-8 per group	A	B	14
Highlight Child	N	3 and up	5-8 per group	Q	B	14-15
Hoop Trains	Y	3-8	Any	A	B	20
Hop-Along	N	5 and up	Any	A	B	57
Hug Tag	Y	6 and up	Any	VA	B	78
Human Bridges or Tunnels	N	4-10	Any	A	B	34-35

Activity name	Equipment	Ages	Number of players	Activity level	Indoors/ outdoors	Page(s)
Human Knot	N	8 and up	Any	Q	B	93
Human Pretzel	N	8 and up	Any	Q	B	93
In and Out	Y	7 and up	Any	A	B	143
Jelly Belly	Y	3 and up	Any	Q	B	71
Jim's Rounders	Y	7 and up	6-8 per team	A	B	106-107
Joy's Inclination	Y	4 and up	Any	A	B	61
Kaipsak (Spinning Tops)	Y	5 and up	Any	A	B	133
Ladder Travel	Y	8 and up	10-12 per group	A	B	90
Line Up by Numbers	Y	4-7	Any	A	B	65
Little People's Big Sack	Y	4 and up	5-16 per sack	A	B	50-51
Log Chute	N	8 and up	Any	A	B	95
Log Roll	N	8 and up	Any	A	B	85-86
Long Log Roll	N	4 and up	Any	A	B	55
Long, Long, Long Jump	N	6 and up	Any	A	B	85
Magic Carpet	Y	4 and up	7-8 per group	VA	B	38
Makii	Y	9 and up	5-8 per team	A	O	129
Manumanu (Little Bird)	Y	8 and up	8-10 per group	A	B	128
Miss Your Legs	Y	9 and up	Any	A	B	143
Muk (Silence)	N	5 and up	Any	A	B	131
No-Elimination Hot Potato	Y	4-10	10-15 per group	Q	B	24

(continued)

Activity name	Equipment	Ages	Number of players	Activity level	Indoors/ outdoors	Page(s)
Nuglutang	Y	8 and up	5-8 per group	A	B	132-133
Object Balance	Y	3 and up	Any	A	B	61
Over and Over	Y	8 and up	Any	A	B	88-89
Parachute	Y	3 and up	12-30 per group	A	B	36-37
Partner Back-Up	N	5 and up	Any	A	B	55
Partner Pull-Up	N	5 and up	Any	A	B	54
Partner Scooter Basketball	Y	8 and up	5-8 pairs per team	A	B	144
Partner Tube Rebounding	Y	5 and up	Any	A	B	75-76
Partners	Y	3-7	Any	VA	B	12
People Machine	N	3-9	4-8 per group	A	B	35-36
Playing Inside the Hoops	Y	3-9	Any	VA	B	19-20
Playing Outside the Hoops	Y	3-9	Any	VA	B	18-19
Positive Yarn	Y	5 and up	6-8 per group	Q	B	48-49
Pot of Gold	Y	5-10	Any	A	B	67
Push 'Em Into Balance	N	7 and up	Any	A	B	81-82
Puzzles	Y	All	2-10 per group	Q	B	45-46
Rescue	Y	4 and up	Any	Q	B	51-52
Rolling Hoops	Y	6 and up	Any	A	B	20
Row Your Boat	Y	4 and up	Any	A	B	75
Scooter Basketball	Y	8 and up	5-8 per team	A	B	144
Scooter Towel Ball	Y	9 and up	5-8 pairs per team	A	B	145

Activity name	Equipment	Ages	Number of players	Activity level	Indoors/ outdoors	Page(s)
Scooter Trains	Y	6 and up	10-15 pairs per group	VA	I	42-44
Secret Message	N	3-8	5-15 per group	Q	B	45
Shapes	N	3-7	2-6 per group	Q	B	46
Sharing Highlights	N	3 and up	5-8 per group	Q	B	13-14
Shoe Twister	Y	4 and up	5-20 per group	Q	B	47-48
Silent Birthday Lineup	N	7 and up	Any	Q	B	90
Simon Says No Elimination	N	4-8	Any	Q	B	23
SoFa Circle Game	N	3-6	Any	Q	B	135
Spaghetti Toes	Y	3 and up	Any	Q	B	71
Special Place Relaxation	Y	5 and up	Any	Q	B	107-108
Spell Sport	Y	7 and up	5-6 per team	A	B	68-69
Spelling Ball	Y	5-9	Any	Q	B	67
Spelling Volley	Y	6 and up	6-10 per team	A	B	68
Spinning Star	N	5-8	4-5 per group	A	B	33
Sticky Popcorn	N	3-7	Any	A	B	35
Stomp and Shake	Y	6 and up	Any	VA	B	76-77
Sum Games	Y	4-9	Any	A	B	65-66
Taketak	Y	9 and up	7-10 per team	A	O	129-130
Target Toss	Y	5-10	Any	A	B	66
The Big Ship Sails	N	3-7	10-20	A	B	63-64
The More We Get Together	N	3-7	10-20	A	B	63

(continued)

Activity name	Equipment	Ages	Number of players	Activity level	Indoors/ outdoors	Page
This Is My Friend	N	3-8	8-12 per group	Q	B	10-11
Thread the Needle	N	4-8	8 per group	A	B	64
Tiptoe Through the Tulips	Y	3-8	5-10 per group	Q	B	49
Toesie Roll	N	3 and up	Any	A	B	58
Togeth-Air Ball (Collective-Score Volleyball)	Y	7 and up	7-10 per side	A	B	97-98
Towering Tower	Y	3-7	Any	A	B	86-87
Tray Balance	Y	3 and up	Any	A	B	60
Tug of Peace: Rope Pull-Up	Y	5 and up	3-4 per group	A	B	57-58
Tug of Peace: Rope Shapes	Y	4 and up	3-4 per group	Q	B	46-47
Tweetie	N	4-7	Any	Q	B	91
Underwater Spelling	Y	8 and up	4-6 per group	A	B	69
Wagon Wheels	N	7 and up	5-7 per group	A	I	32
Wand Balance	Y	5-8	Any	A	B	60
Water Bridge	N	7 and up	Any	A	B	95
Water Cup Pass	Y	7 and up	Any	Q	O	94
Water-Balloon Toss	Y	6 and up	Any	A	O	96
Watermelon Split	Y	8 and up	Any	A	B	83
What Can You Do Together?	N	3 and up	Any	A/Q	B	52-53
What's the Action?	Y	7 and up	4-5 per group	A	B	69
Whirlpool	N	7 and up	Any	A	B	96
Wring the Dishrag	N	7 and up	Any	A	B	56

1

Who Needs Cooperative Games?

Have you ever seen the fun torn from a child in a game? Have you ever seen children left out, put down, rejected, or intentionally hurt in games? Have you ever thought that there must be a better way? Then the games in this book are for you! They have grown out of these concerns and provide a positive alternative. What's so different about these games? They are games of acceptance, cooperation, and joy that can bring children, families, and communities together in the spirit of cooperative play. They have been carefully created, selected, and refined so that children have fun while learning positive things about themselves, about others, and about how we should be in the world.

The main advantages of cooperative games are that everybody cooperates . . . everybody wins . . . and everybody has fun. Children play with one another rather than against one another. These games eliminate the fear and feeling of failure. They nurture and reaffirm a child's confidence or value in himself or herself as an acceptable and worthy person. In competitive games, personal acceptance and joy are often awarded to just one winner. In cooperative games, these elements are designed into the games themselves.

My goal throughout this book is to enhance the quality of children's lives by enhancing the quality of children's early experiences with play and games. Cooperative games provide beautiful occasions for collaboration, challenge, stimulation, self-validation, success, and sheer fun. This is what cooperative games are all about.

Some cultures have played games cooperatively for centuries. However, very few games are designed specifically so that all players—children or adults—strive toward one common, mutually desirable goal. Cooperative games (games with no losers) are extremely rare. Their rediscovery is something we can look forward to and gain from. Children live what they learn in their play and games. The lessons they learn should drive human values and human interaction in the most positive direction possible.

The first cooperative games that I encountered in other cultures were ones that I played with the Inuit (Eskimos) in remote regions of the Canadian Arctic and with the aboriginal people in remote regions of Papua New Guinea and the Australian outback. These experiences influenced my vision of what games could be, and I set out on a journey to create my own cooperative games. The cooperative games in this book came primarily from my own work and play with children, students, teachers, parents, and grandparents from many different parts of the world, over a period of more than three decades.

The beauty of these games lies in the values they promote—inclusion, cooperation, empathy, and fun—and in their versatility and adaptability. For the most part, cooperative games require little or no equipment and virtually no outlay of cash. They can be used with a range of populations and in a variety of physical settings. Anyone can play them, almost anywhere. The rules of the specific games need not be strictly followed. You can work out your own specific details. You don't need a certain kind of ball to play with or a specific kind of field to play on. You don't even need to play in predetermined positions or for preset time periods. These things really don't matter. The important thing is the concept behind the games.

The games presented throughout this book have been designed and field tested with children. At certain age levels, patience may be needed in order to teach this "new" form of play, particularly if the participants have never before played cooperatively. However, with appropriate challenges, enlightened supervision, repeated exposure, and players' constructive input on cooperative changes, the games will begin to take on a positive life of their own. Once people make the transition and begin to play cooperatively—and for fun—supervision and concerns about rules usually become minimal. The players begin to supervise and officiate their own behavior and also become concerned about one another's safety.

Cooperative games are not restricted to children. Many teenagers and adults like to revisit their childhood or lift their adult lives momentarily through some of these fun-filled ventures. Many of these cooperative activities have also been used successfully as icebreakers or team-building activities with sports teams, business groups, work teams, and university students as well as with people at conferences and parties.

The age categories outlined for the games should serve only as a rough guide. Specific game selections or adaptations can easily be made by children, adolescents, and adults of all ages to ensure that the games are (and continue to be) appropriately suited to the specific needs of the group.

THE NEED FOR POSITIVE ALTERNATIVES

Children's games began as sanctuaries for joyful, playful human interaction. Play served as a wonderful medium for teaching children how to interact in positive ways with one another and the world around them. The joy that was once a natural part of children's games has been replaced with something more rigid, judgmental, and outcome oriented. Too often there is pressure to perform, with no escape from being evaluated. Within these contexts, fear of failure and stress about not being good enough are heightened. In the end, the shift in focus away from joyful, playful, cooperative interaction toward squeezing the most out of each child leaves little room for plain old fun. Cooperative games are designed to remove the stress and put the fun back into children's games.

If children's early experiences with games and sport are positive, joyful, and uplifting, then more children will become joyfully engaged in physical activity and sport over the course of their lifetimes. If they feel good and valued within the activity, they will want to continue with it. If they feel bad or rejected, there is a very good chance they will not want to continue. Early feelings of failure in games or sport often result in children's opting out of physically oriented pursuits, which can also result in lowering children's overall self-esteem. Children spend a great deal of time playing in their developmental years. We owe it to them to make those experiences as joyful and life enhancing as they can possibly be for every child.

When children play cooperative games, they almost always feel a sense of acceptance, joy, contribution, and success. We need more games and sports programs in which all children feel accepted and experience at least a moderate degree of success. When children think they have done

Play should be joyful, inclusive, and life enhancing for every child.

well or contributed or won, there is no need for them to feel threatened or anxious and every reason to feel happy with themselves and the experience. The fear and stress associated with failure are reduced when errors are not viewed as a life-and-death matter. In cooperative activities, there are no losers. The friendly, low-key competition reduces the importance of outcome, freeing children to enjoy each other and the experience of playing itself. Participants are given a new freedom to learn from their mistakes rather than fear them or hide them. When children know that their value as persons will not be shattered by the outcome of an event or the score in a game, then games and playmates can be approached in a new, more positive light. Our goal is to give every child a firm base of joy, cooperation, and acceptance from which to start.

Four essential components make up a successful cooperative game: cooperation, acceptance, inclusion, and fun.

Why Cooperation?

Cooperation, caring, and collaboration are critical skills for living our lives fully and joyfully, both as children and as adults. Most of what we do in life involves interacting with other people. Think of your own life. When is your life with other people most joyful or most productive—at home, at school, at work, at play, in personal relationships, or in interactions of any context? It is probably when people are cooperating—caring, listening, collaborating, and being respectful. When is your life with other people least joyful or least productive? It is probably when people are not cooperating—not caring, not listening, not collaborating, and not being respectful.

Joy and success within personal relationships and working relationships (e.g., teaching, coaching, managing, or working with clients) are dependent on having skills that free us to interact in positive and cooperative ways—caring, listening, collaborating, empathizing, and being respectful. If we lack the basic skills for cooperating and interacting with others in positive and respectful ways, we will never bring out the best in ourselves or the best in others, regardless of the depth of our technical, academic, or experiential knowledge. People who lack skills for cooperation and empathy put themselves and others at a great disadvantage in living their lives fully and joyfully and in making truly meaningful contributions. This is one of the reasons I believe it is so important to teach children cooperative skills and respectful perspectives at an early age—so they can carry these skills with them for the rest of their lives.

Think of your own children and the children with whom you work or play. When are your children's lives with other children (or other adults) most joyful? It is probably when they are cooperating, caring, and being respectful. When are your children's lives with other children (or adults) least joyful? It is probably when they are not cooperating, not caring, and not being respectful.

Cooperation is clearly one of the most important and least developed of all human skills. Most conflicts at the individual, team, and societal level occur when people do not have the will or skills for caring and cooperating. The majority of problems we encounter in our families, personal relationships, games, schools, work, communities, and world are related to a lack of genuine caring, respect, and cooperation. A perspective that is both respectful and cooperative leads to more empathy, better communication, increased cohesiveness, higher levels of trust, and the development of better people—people who care about their performances, their contributions, and other people.

Cooperative play and games provide an ideal medium for teaching children skills for cooperation, caring, and collaboration. They also provide a wonderful opportunity for practicing the skills of cooperation and experiencing its value. Through cooperative play, children learn to share, to empathize with others, to be concerned about others' feelings, to help each other, to work together to achieve a common goal, to get along better, and to enjoy each other's company. The players in cooperative games help one another by working together as a unit—each player being a necessary part of that unit, with a contribution to make—and leaving no one to feel left out of the action or to sit around waiting for a chance to play. The fact that children work together toward a common end, rather than against one another, immediately turns destructive responses into helpful ones. Players believe they are an accepted part of the game, contributors in the game, and thus feel totally involved. The result is an experience of gaining, not losing.

Everyone gains from learning and perfecting skills for respectful cooperation. We gain most by learning these skills at an early age. This way, children have their whole lives to use and refine these essential human skills. And when children begin to learn these skills at an early age, those of us who are parents, teachers, coaches, friends, and members of the community also have the rest of our lives to benefit from these children's more positive interactions.

Why Acceptance?

Feelings of acceptance are directly related to heightened self-esteem and overall happiness—just as rejection is directly related to a decline in self-esteem and feelings of despair. In cooperative games, each child plays a meaningful role within the game, once she chooses to become involved. Each child is also at least partially responsible for the accomplishment of the goal or successful outcome of the game. In cooperative games, children feel accepted. After playing cooperative games for the first time, an 8-year-old girl came running over to me and said, "I love these games because in cooperative games I feel left in." This is one of our goals—for children to feel "left in" because this makes them feel good about themselves and good about their teammates.

Why Inclusion?

Inclusion in enjoyable physical activity is important for living a balanced, healthy, and joyful life—at all age levels. Children's early experiences with physical activity are extremely important because this is when they usually develop a love for physical activity or an aversion to it. Positive inclusion in cooperative games and other enjoyable physical activities is directly related to feelings of belonging, to a sense of contribution and satisfaction with the activity. When children feel left out, pushed out, eliminated, or ignored, they clearly "feel it" as a form of rejection. Children want to be part of the action, not apart from it. This genuine desire for inclusion and acceptance is fully respected in cooperative games. Children are freed from worries about being humiliated or rejected, and everyone is fully included.

Why Fun?

We should never lose sight of the fact that the primary reason children play games at all is to have fun. When you keep the fun in the game, you nourish the heart and soul of the child. When you take the fun out

In cooperative games, children feel "left in."

of a game, you rip the joy out of the child, and you remove the child's primary reason for being there. In cooperative games, fun is enhanced as children are freed to play with others for fun, without fear of failure or rejection and without any need for destructiveness. Children are free to adapt the games to make them even more fun. Sharing heightens the fun experience.

When these four components—cooperation, acceptance, inclusion, and fun—are combined to create a child's game, there are no more wounded self-concepts, no more hurt feelings, no more reasons for tears or fear. All children are free to enjoy the game and to leave the game feeling enriched by the experience. Within the context of the game, the children are living the experience of being positive, being in the moment, and being joyful. And through this process they learn something of value about how to cooperate with others, how to respect others, and how to live their lives joyfully. What better purpose could a child's game serve?

PUTTING COOPERATIVE IDEAS INTO ACTION

Cooperative Games and Sports is a book about action—putting good cooperative ideas into action! The games in this book can be played by all kinds of people—young and old—in a variety of settings: your house or apartment, birthday parties, play days, picnics, gym classes, camps, preschools, classrooms, community centers, exercise groups, work parties, company retreats, hospitals, senior citizen homes, therapy settings, treatment or detention centers, and so on. When playing the various games in this book, remember that it is not necessary to follow every single detail precisely. A certain amount of detail is necessary to get you going, but beyond that, flexibility should be the rule so that the games remain fluid to the participants' needs and do not become too rigid.

You will probably find that some cooperative games will work extremely well for your purposes, and others might not work as well. Once you become familiar with the concept underlying cooperative activities, you can begin to adapt some games and hopefully invent some new ones that best meet the needs of your particular children, client group, or situation. If your heart is in the right place, I am certain that you will do a great job introducing these games to others and coming up with some very good activities on your own. Have fun with the process.

BUILDING ON THE UNIQUENESS OF THESE COOPERATIVE ACTIVITIES

As you read through and play the games presented on the following pages, I encourage you to think beyond the specific game—to the concept behind the game. These games are designed to teach children the value of cooperation, teamwork, and joyful interaction. They are designed to promote positive human interaction and to nurture respectful human values. As you explore these unique cooperative activities, keep in mind that the concept behind them is what makes them unique. This same respectful concept can be integrated into many different contexts, including the home, the classroom, the gym, the outdoors, and the workplace.

Cooperative games can get you and your children or students moving in a positive direction, and you can adapt or create additional positively oriented activities for different contexts and age groups. You have the capacity to change the underlying orientation of almost any game, activity, or pursuit to elicit more genuine cooperation and a higher level of respectful interaction. You have the capacity to find, and help others find, opportunities for positive interaction and personal growth in almost any situation or context. My initial goal in writing this book was for you to play these games with your children. My deeper goal is for you and your children to see, understand, and live the respectful values underlying these games. If you take this orientation into your life, you will get the most out of it.

2 Games for Children Ages 3 Through 7

Children in this age range like lots of variety but also enjoy getting to know a few games very well and playing them over and over again. They seem to like a mix of very active and quiet games, some challenging and others with very little challenge at all.

Children aged 3 to 7 have fun playing the following cooperative games and will quickly learn how to work together as a unit if the games are broken down into clear and simple steps. Within weeks of directed cooperative play, we often see positive spin-offs of increased cooperation within the games and outside the games in their daily activities.

Note that there is nothing sacred about the age category suggested for these games. Although we tested the games with children aged 3 to 7 and found them well received, many games are perfectly acceptable or adaptable for 8- to 12-year-olds and even teenagers and adults. So stay flexible and open-minded when thinking about how to use these games and with whom.

NAME GAMES

Cooperative name games are an excellent way to begin cooperative activity sessions with young children. We usually start with This Is My Friend. This game helps us get to know the children's names and helps the children get to know each other's names.

This Is My Friend

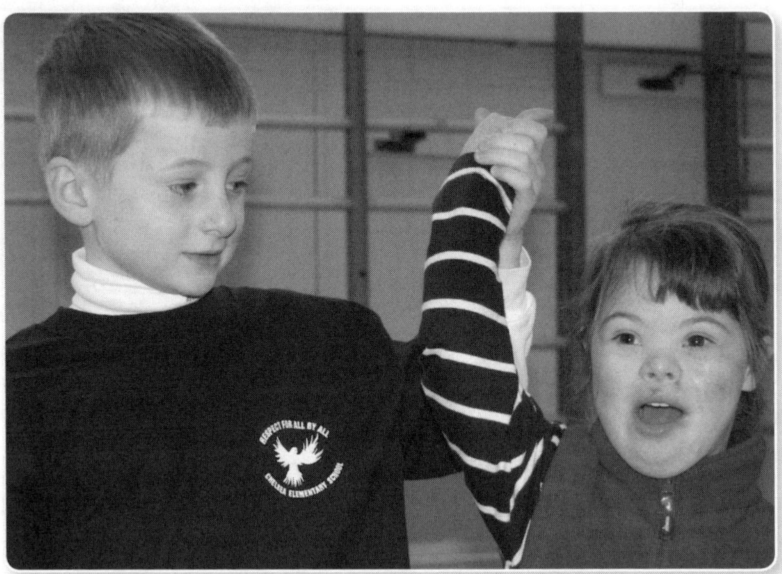

Description

1. Children begin the game by sitting in a circle. Ask them to find out the name of the child sitting on their immediate left. If they already know that child's name, they do not have to ask. If they do not know that child's name, they simply ask him.
2. Everyone in the circle then joins hands, and the name game begins. One child starts the game by introducing the person on his left to the rest of the group, using a *big* voice so everyone can hear: "This is my friend John." When he says his friend's name ("John"), he raises John's hand in the air. John then introduces the person on his left in the same way and raises her hand. This continues until everyone has been introduced.

Variations

- Another way to play this game is for each child in the circle to pair up with the child sitting next to her. Both children in a pair stand up and take turns raising the other child's hand in the air, saying her name out loud. After the introductions, they both sit back down in the circle, and the next pair of children stands up.
- Once the children are familiar with the name game and know each other's names, they can begin to share positive things they like about their friends or ask simple questions to gain additional positive information to share with others (e.g., "This is my friend Barbara. I like her because she is nice to me. She has a dog. She likes painting."). Ask the children to discover and share one thing they like about the friend sitting next to them in the circle that day or one thing that friend likes to do. Adapt this approach for older groups by giving participants four or five minutes to find out as many positive things as possible about their new acquaintances (or something new about old friends). They then introduce their friends to the group. When adults play the name game, we often ask them to find out what their new friends love to do, what makes them feel most fully alive, and what they are most proud of.

Helpful Tip

We have played this game successfully with 5-, 6-, and 7-year-olds, and it even works with preschool children with a little prompting and patience. Many young children have never before introduced anyone else. Up until this time, introductions have always been a "me" thing. People have introduced young children to others, but young children have rarely introduced another person or shared things they like about another person. Once they get the spirit and routine of starting a session with this game, every time they come into the gym or play area, they immediately go to the center of the room and play their little introduction game before moving on to other cooperative ventures.

Gesture Name Game

Description

In this game, children introduce themselves in a way that is active and fun. This cooperative game revolves around names and also involves the need to focus on remembering names and movements.

1. The children begin by standing in a circle. Each player in turn introduces herself by making a gesture as she says each syllable in her

name. For example, while Jane Snowshoe is saying, "Jane," she raises both her hands high in the air. When she says, "Snowshoe," she stamps one foot with the first syllable ("Snow") and the other foot with the second syllable ("shoe").

2. Together the group then says, "Hello, Jane Snowshoe," repeating her name and acting out the gestures. Then it's on to the second person.

Helpful Tip

Encourage children to remember the other children's names and gestures for the next game. Some children may then be able to introduce their friend (e.g., "This is my friend Jane Snowshoe") and include the gestures. The other children then repeat the name and gestures.

Partners

Equipment

A stereo and CD or other way of playing music

Description

1. Four-year-olds start this game by holding hands with one partner. When you play the music, the children run, hop, skip, or twirl around the room or play area while linked with a partner.
2. When you stop the music, they "freeze" where they are.
3. Start the music again to "unfreeze" the children, letting them skip around the room again with one or more partners. They often end up linked to many partners.

Variations

- The 5-, 6-, and 7-year-olds usually start by scooting around the room on their own. On the signal "Partners," they quickly find a nearby partner, hold hands, and "freeze" together on the spot. After dropping hands, one child becomes the actor and the other becomes a "mirror," imitating whatever the actor child does. Each partner takes a turn being the actor and the mirror. The children then run around the room again until they hear "Partners." This time each child finds a new partner.
- Introductions ("Howdy, partner. I'm Terry. What's your name?" or "What's your favorite game?") can be incorporated into this game to help children get to know one another better.

HIGHLIGHT GAMES

I have been playing highlight games with children and adults for many years, and based on these experiences, I believe that sharing highlights is one of the most important and uplifting activities we can engage in to enrich the quality of our lives. Let me tell you more about highlights. Think about the things you love or like to do. Think of the best parts of your day. Think of the simple things that can lift you each day and make your day feel that it was worth living. These are highlights, and they are within your grasp. Highlights are things you can do or experience over and over again and still find joy in them. Our highlight games encourage children to think about the good things in their day and the good things in their lives. They remind children to appreciate and live the simple joys every day. A day without highlights is a day without joy, so it is important to go treasure hunting for highlights every day. The value of playing these games becomes obvious as soon as you start playing them.

Sharing Highlights

Description

This first highlight game is a simple game of sharing highlights. It can be played in any setting or context with same-age groups or mixed-age groups. Players sit in a circle on the floor or around a table and think of a highlight from today or the last couple of days. One person begins by sharing a highlight. Move around the circle, giving every child a chance to share a highlight. One of the following questions can be used to get things rolling: "Tell us one thing that made you feel happy or good or proud yesterday or today." "What was the best part of your day?" It is an uplifting experience to hear each child talk about good things, happy things—highlights.

Variation

Other ways to share highlights or fill a room with highlights include asking the children to draw their highlights, write them down, or bring in pictures of their highlights.

Helpful Tips

- Sharing highlights on a regular basis reminds us to look for highlights, find highlights, create highlights, and share highlights. "How many highlights did you have today?" "How many highlights will you have tomorrow?"
- Sharing highlights is a great way to end the day on a positive note in almost any context—at school, at camp, after a sports event,

at work, or at home. Try going around the table at home after dinner and letting each person share his highlights of the day. It is a very positive and uplifting activity for all. Try it!

Highlight Charades

Description

People of all ages can play this game. To begin, ask the children (or adults) to get into groups of five or six to share their highlights. Then ask them to pick one of the highlights to act out as a group so that other groups can guess what it is. Give them a few minutes to decide how their group will act out the highlight (with everyone playing some part and no one talking). This game can also be played in pairs or small groups, with each child acting out her own highlight for a partner or the rest of the group to guess. Children enjoy playing this game, and it has important benefits outside the game as well. The more they hear, see, and share highlights, the more ideas they get for how they can live with more highlights each day. We have also found that as children increase the number of highlights they experience each day, they feel better about themselves (higher self-esteem) and are happier overall. My *Positive Living Skills for Children* audio CDs contain some excellent stories designed specifically to help children find more joy and highlights every day (see Resources, page 160, for further information). I often play these CD activities for children in classes I teach, in play groups, at home, and in the car. I find them extremely effective.

Highlight Child

Description

This version is played the same way as the original game Sharing Highlights, except the focus is on finding qualities or highlights in other people. In this game, each player shares something he loves, appreciates, respects, or admires in another person.

One way to play is to start with one highlight child and let each other child in the group share one thing she likes or admires about that person. Then move to the next highlight child, giving everyone a chance to share a quality he likes about that child.

Variations

- We usually play this game in small groups, but it can be played with entire sports teams, class teams, or work teams.

- Another option for playing this game is to let children share good things they like or love about anyone they know. "Who is a person that makes you feel really good?" "What does that person do or say that makes you feel good or special or valued?" "What is it that makes you love or like or admire that person?" The person a child talks about could be someone in his circle, class, play group, or school; a person on her team or another team; or a friend, teacher, coach, or family member.

BALLOON GAMES

Young children love playing cooperative games with balloons. Colorful balloons create a party atmosphere for children—no matter where they are. I always use balloons when introducing the idea of working together with groups of young children to ensure that their first experience is uplifting and fun.

Balloon Keep-Up

Equipment

One balloon for every two children (have some extra balloons inflated in case any pop during the game; larger balloons work best because they stay up in the air longer)

Description

1. The children pair up, and each pair is given an inflated balloon. Their first goal is to see if they can throw or tap the balloon back and forth to each other, with each partner catching and throwing or hitting the balloon once. This introduces the idea of a common goal and the importance of taking turns.
2. Then ask players to see if (or how long) they can tap the balloon back and forth without letting it fall to the floor or ground. This introduces the idea of a collective goal. If the balloon touches the floor, they just pick it up and begin tapping it back and forth again. Kids love to do this simple cooperative activity.

Variations

- For an additional challenge for preschoolers, Balloon Keep-Up can be played in groups of three. Three children try to keep one balloon in the air, with each taking her turn. Another fun option is to give each child a balloon. Partners sit (or stand) facing each other, and both children throw their own balloons into the air at about the same time. They try to catch their partner's balloon before it touches the ground. Then they repeat the balloon exchange process.

- For additional challenge, older children can count the number of consecutive hits before the balloon touches the floor or play the game in small groups of three or four, with each child taking a turn, while in different formations (circle, square).
- For a cooperative challenge without a score, partners or groups of three can work together to keep a balloon in the air with alternate hand hits while moving from one end of the play area to the other or while going through an obstacle course (over walls, through tunnels, and so on) or can attempt to keep a balloon up outdoors in the wind or rain or with the aid of an implement such as a paper plate or cardboard fan.

Cooperative Balloons Through Hoops

Equipment

One balloon and one hula hoop per four children

Description

Once the children are able to tap a balloon back and forth several times in a row, they are ready for this more challenging balloon activity. It takes a little practice and a lot of cooperation, but children enjoy playing this game.

Two pairs of children team up. Give each team of four children one balloon and one hula hoop. One set of partners holds the hoop up at waist level, close to the floor, or above their heads (perpendicular to the ground), each holding one side of the hoop. The other set of partners tries to tap, hit, or throw the balloon back and forth through the upright hoop. Partners rotate from tapping the balloon back and forth to holding the stationary hoop.

Variation

With older children, consider substituting beach balls for balloons. Younger children have more success starting with balloons because they stay up in the air longer, giving players a better chance of getting to the balloon before it falls to the ground.

Helpful Tip

Tell the children that everyone is needed to make the game successful, and remind them to focus on doing their jobs—watching the balloon, hitting the balloon, or holding the hoop straight so the balloon has a better chance of going through the hoop. Encourage them to help one another, coach one another, and cheer for one another.

Beach-Ball Balance

Equipment

One beach ball or balloon per two children

Description

In this game, two children share one beach ball or balloon, trying to hold the ball between them without using their hands. Ask them to see how many ways they can balance the beach ball between them (head to head, side to side, back to back, and so on) and to move around the room holding the ball in different ways. With the ball balanced forehead to

forehead, they can both attempt to bend forward to touch their knees, squat down, and so on. The children can also attempt to step through a hanging hula hoop or obstacle course while remaining connected by the beach ball. Alternatively, they can try to balance two or three balls between them or balance the balls in groups of three and four and so on.

Variations

- A 5-year-old boy suggested trying to balance all the balls between all the children. Naturally we tried it. The younger children weren't totally successful, but they had a lot of fun in the process, and some older groups were able to do it. Other variations include having partners try to pick up a beach ball or balloon off the floor using heads only or backs only or to form a circle and try to pass a series of beach balls or balloons from one set of partners to another without using their hands.
- Beach-Ball Train: Some of our 6-year-old children were successful in making beach-ball and balloon trains by standing in a line and placing a beach ball or balloon between each person. Many children can link up in this manner to make a big train that can move around the play area. Some of our 7-year-olds tried to hold beanbags (which you can buy or make yourself) between their bodies while moving around the gym and through an obstacle course. This provides an interesting challenge and certainly brings the children into close contact.

HOOP GAMES

Hula hoops are a wonderful play medium for creating a variety of fun-filled cooperative activities for children. The circular plastic hoops provide an ideal structure within which two or more children can play together, making hula hoops a very effective means of promoting initial cooperation among young children.

Playing Outside the Hoops

Equipment

One hula hoop per two children; a stereo and CD or other way of playing music

Description

1. Begin by dividing the group into pairs, with each pair of children sitting outside a hoop on the floor.

2. To start the game the children stand up outside their hoop, facing the same direction, with one child on each side of the hoop. Each child holds on to his side with one hand.
3. When you play the music, the children walk, skip, or run around the play area, making sure they do not bump into anyone else. They can experiment with different ways to move around the play area at the same pace. For example, partners can remain side by side, or one child can move to the front of the hoop, facing forward with his hands behind him, while his partner moves to the back of the hoop and holds the hoop with her hands in front of her—like a horse in front with a driver or jockey in the back.

Helpful Tip

Ask the children to be very quiet and to focus on listening to the instructions on how to play the game. Attentive listening and respect for others (adults and other children) are important parts of what we are trying to teach within the cooperative games context. The children should try to focus with their eyes, minds, and bodies while the game is being introduced. Emphasize that they have to respect their partners by playing together and respect the other children by sharing the same play space.

Playing Inside the Hoops

Equipment

One hula hoop per two children; a stereo and CD or other way of playing music

Description

1. Begin by dividing the group into pairs, with each pair of children sitting inside a hoop on the floor. Ask the children to be very quiet and to focus on listening to the instructions on how to play the game.

2. To begin the game, the children stand up inside their hoop, facing the same direction, and hold the hoop, usually at waist or shoulder level. Each child holds up her portion of the hoop.
3. When you play the music, the children skip around the room, staying inside their hoop.
4. Each time the music stops, children from two different hoops team up by stacking their hoops together and getting inside them. This process continues until as many children as possible are all together inside (and holding up) as many stacked hoops as possible. The game generally ends with about six or eight children moving slowly in one hoop, depending on age level.

Helpful Tip

Remind the children that to play this game successfully, when they are inside the hoops, they must work together to move in the same direction and at the same time and pace.

Hoop Trains

Equipment

One hula hoop per two children

Description

Two children pair up inside each hoop and then attempt to make a hoop train by connecting with other pairs of children who remain inside their own hoops. Present them with the challenge of making a big hoop train, and let them figure out how to do it.

Rolling Hoops

Equipment

One hula hoop per two children

Description

This game works well with slightly older children. Children pair up and attempt to roll their hoop back and forth to each other. Once they are successful at rolling the hoop back and forth, they can team up with another pair of children who try to throw a beach ball or beanbag through the hoop as it is rolling. Partners take turns rolling and throwing.

NO-ELIMINATION GAMES

No child likes to be eliminated from a game or cut from a team. The following games show you how to turn children's games of elimination into no-elimination games of joy and inclusion.

Cooperative Musical Chairs

Equipment

One chair per player (minus one); a stereo and CD or other way of playing music

Description

One of the first cooperative games I created was Cooperative Musical Chairs. The way I changed this game from its original competitive design illustrates a basic difference in orientation between cooperative games and competitive games. In the original competitive version of Musical Chairs, each child begins by sitting on a chair in a long line of chairs. When music is played, all the children get up and skip or run around the chairs, and one chair is removed. When the music stops, all the children scramble to try to sit on one of the remaining chairs. Because there is one fewer chair than there are children, one child is necessarily eliminated from the game. She or he is told to go to the side of the room and sit on the floor.

Each time the music plays, another chair is removed and another child is eliminated. She or he also sits on the side while the game continues: playing the music, removing one chair, stopping the music, and eliminating another child, until one child—the winner—is left on the chair and all the others are left out sitting on the sidelines.

I have watched young children play the competitive version of Musical Chairs on many occasions and witnessed their tears and looks of despair as each one is eliminated from the game. If 20 children start out playing the game, 19 will be eliminated. The game is designed to eliminate children by ensuring that they do not find a chair. Games of elimination are totally inappropriate for young children. Children need games of inclusion, not games of rejection.

In Cooperative Musical Chairs, the game is designed to keep everyone included even though chairs are systematically removed. This simple change makes a huge difference in how the game is played.

1. As in the competitive version, set up as many chairs as you need, one for each player minus one (i.e., if you have 20 players, you should have 19 chairs). Have a stereo and CD on hand so you can play music.
2. Play the music, then stop it. When the music stops, all players try to sit on one of the chairs. Because there are more children than chairs, players have to be creative and team up so that every player is sitting on the chairs available to keep everyone in the game. Players can meet this challenge in a number of creative ways, such as sharing the remaining chairs, sitting on each other, leaning on each other, or being in contact with other children who are either sitting on a chair or in contact with someone who is sitting on a chair.
3. Remove a chair, and start the music again. Repeat the process, removing one chair at a time so that all players work together to sit on fewer chairs.
4. In the end, all 20 children who started the game are delicately perched on one, two, three, or four chairs (depending on age level), as opposed to 19 disappointed children standing on the sidelines with one "winner" on one chair.

Variation

To play Cooperative Musical Hoops, children skip around hula hoops spread out on the floor. When you stop the music, the children jump inside one of the hoops. After every round, remove one hoop. All the children must work together to ensure that everyone (or some part of everyone) becomes part of the remaining hoops. It is sometimes easier to play with hoops than with chairs because hoops are easier to lift, move around, and store.

Helpful Tip

If you play this game with children outside in a park and no chairs or hoops are available, adults or teenagers on their hands and knees can serve as chairs, or they can form hoops by lying down on the ground in a circle linking hands to feet. If no music is available, the human chairs or human hoops can sing and together decide when their "music" stops and which human chairs or human hoops will remain until the end of the game.

Simon Says No Elimination

Description

One of my early game adaptations designed to eliminate the elimination of children was a remake of Simon Says. In the original competitive version of this game, a leader stands in front of a group of children and performs various movements that the children try to mimic when given the command "Simon says do this." When the leader says, "Do this," without first having said, "Simon says," any child who follows is eliminated from the game and sits on the side of the room while the remaining children continue to play. This continues until all but one child is eliminated (or until the allotted time for the game runs out).

In the cooperative version of Simon Says, two games begin simultaneously, each with a leader who performs various movements that the children try to mimic when given the command "Simon says do this." However in this version, when the leader says, "Do this," without first having said, "Simon says," any child who follows merely transfers to the other game, joining in the next Simon Says. There is no exclusion, only movement back and forth between two parallel games. This gives every child the opportunity to keep playing and to keep learning the skills that allow every child to remain in the game. Why Simon failed to say, "No one will be left out of this game!" before now is a mystery to me.

Variation

Simon Says No Elimination can also be played in pairs where children take turns leading each other.

No-Elimination Hot Potato

Equipment

A beanbag or ball

Description

1. The children join hands and sit down to form a potato-passing circle.
2. A hot potato (beanbag or ball) is passed around the circle from one person to the next until the potato caller (who starts as the only person in a separate potato-callers' circle) shouts, "Hot potato!" The person holding the potato at this time jumps up and runs to join the potato-callers' circle. He chooses a number, to which the callers count softly together before yelling, "Hot potato!" in unison.
3. The game continues in this manner until the last child remains in the potato-passing circle. The child passes the hot potato back and forth from one hand to the other until the other children yell "hot potato." Then she switches to the potato-callers' circle where all the other children have had a chance to select a number to count to. This child becomes the first potato caller for the next game. It is interesting to note that the children have no sense of losing in this game. They enjoy being in either circle because both circles are "in."

Freeing Your Friends

Equipment

One beanbag for each child

Description

1. This is an active game of helping. All the children begin by moving around the gym or play area at their own pace, each balancing a beanbag on his head.
2. Change the action or pace by asking the children to move faster, skip, hop, go backward, go slower, turn around, and so on.
3. If the beanbag falls off a child's head, she is frozen and must remain motionless. Another child can pick up that child's beanbag and replace it to free her, without losing his own beanbag.

4. At the end of the game, ask the children questions such as "How many of you helped your friends?" "How many times did you help your friends?" "How did you feel when you helped someone else?" "How did you feel when someone helped you?"

Helpful Tip

This is a good game for 6-, 7-, and 8-year-olds and can be a lot of fun when played to music. While helping another, 5-year-olds can hold on to their own beanbag instead of balancing it on their heads. Remind the children that the objective of the game is to help their friends by freeing them and keeping them in the game.

ANIMAL GAMES

Young children love to play animal games where they draw upon their vivid imaginations to become all sorts of wonderful creatures that do lots of cool things. The following games will take them along their path in a cooperative way.

Barnyard

Description

This fun game can be adapted for any age level. When we played this game one fine spring day with 5-year-olds, we thought we had added only one group of frogs. We soon realized that two separate groups of frogs had formed. With all the seriousness a 5-year-old could muster, little Anna blurted out, "We better decide if a frog goes 'ribbit' or 'croak.'"

1. For young children I often begin by whispering the name of different animals to different players. For example, to end up with three groups of animals, I might whisper the word *cow* to a third of the children, *wolf* to another third of the children, and *snake* to the remaining children.
2. The players then scatter themselves around the room, shut their eyes, turn themselves around in a circle a couple of times, and then begin making their animal sound. The objective of the game is for the children to listen for their animal sound so they can find all the members of their group and then link arms with them.
3. The only means of communication allowed is the animal sound—and it's OK if they peek a little!

Variations

- Another option for children (and adults) is to let each group choose their own animal sound or their own group sound that will allow them to regroup with their eyes closed. After each group has decided on their own sound, everyone spreads out around the play area, closes her eyes, turns around three times, and begins to try to regroup by sound. There is a lot of laughter in this game, and it is also fun to watch.
- When I have six or more groups of animals, I often let half of those groups watch the other groups who are making their sounds. Then they switch roles so those who were playing get a chance to watch the others try to regroup by sound alone.
- You and your children can create many variations for this game. For example, you might stipulate that each group must end up with three cows, three snakes, and three wolves. Groups of linked animals can also be assigned other challenges such as finding the sleeping, snoring farmer or the lost sheep (who are stationary but can make soft sounds) or finding their "den," which can be designated by a stuffed animal, a large mat, or a coiled rope.
- Other alternatives include playing with eyes wide open and voices silent. Each person imitates his animal's movements and can claim as his mates other people imitating the same animal. Pairs or groups of similar animals can link up and move around the room together. Each group can guess what the other groups of animals are.

Caterpillar Over the Mountain

Equipment

Something children can use to create a small "mountain" to crawl over (such as a bench or play blocks); "grass" to cover the mountain (e.g., a mat or sleeping pad)

Description

1. First the children work together either to construct a mountain or to move it into place. The mountain can be made using a wooden bench, large play blocks, a small boat turned upside down, a log, or anything else that appeals to them. Once the children have helped build or move the mountain (which even the youngest group is fully capable of doing when they cooperate), they again work together to put the grass on top of the mountain. A mat or thin sleeping pad draped over the mountain makes good grass.
2. To form the caterpillar, the children line up on their hands and knees and hold the ankles of the child in front of them. Four children can form one 16-legged caterpillar, which moves around the room and over the mountain.
3. Caterpillars can link up with other caterpillars until one giant caterpillar is formed, which crawls over the mountain and slides down the other side. A whole-class caterpillar may need more than one mountain to crawl over.

4. Caterpillars can also coil up and go to sleep or crawl into a cocoon.

Variations

- If you have the time and the creative energy, you could make a caterpillar-like cover with a fuzzy head and lots of little sewn-on feet (and peepholes or holes for little hands to fit through), within which the children maneuver and even exchange places. This would be particularly appropriate for 3-, 4-, and 5-year-olds.
- For those interested in becoming more elaborate, Chinese dragons or horses that require several children to operate can also be used. A big, colorful head with material draped behind can be many things and can even go through a human obstacle course (e.g., under human legs, over human arms, between human bellies).

Big Turtle

Equipment

Something children can use for a "turtle shell" (a lightweight gym mat works fine as a shell; use your imagination for other materials, such as a large sheet of cardboard, a blanket, a thin mattress, or a camping pad)

Description

A group of about seven or eight children get on their hands and knees under a large "turtle shell" and try to make the turtle move in one direction.

Variations

- Six- and 7-year-old children can have fun trying to get the turtle to go over a mountain (a sturdy bench with a mat draped over it will do just fine) or through an obstacle course without losing the shell.
- Five-year-olds enjoy playing this game with the theme of "the tortoise and the hare"; as in the fable, the tortoise follows a steady, straight line and the hare (three little people hopping together) zigzags all over the place.

Helpful Tip

Remember that meaningful cooperative work with young children takes time, and if you stick with it and are persistent, it will work. When we first tried this activity with 5-year-olds, the children under the shell all moved in different directions, and the turtle shell dropped to the floor. But before long they realized that they had to work together to get the whole turtle to move. When we first tried it with 4-year-olds, as soon as the shell was placed on their collective backs, the children all lay down, curled up, and pretended they were sleeping. After carefully explaining to them that if the sleeping turtle was going to move, they needed to stay on their hands and knees, they looked at us with those big 4-year-old eyes. So we heaved the turtle shell upon their backs with great anticipation. What did they do? They all lay down again. I had a flash of a title for a new book or movie: *The Return of the Sleeping Turtle.* We weren't ready to give up yet, so we tried having the turtle move around without its shell (cooperative crawling in one direction). This worked fine. I thought to myself, *This time when the shell is moved into place, it's for sure going to work.* It didn't! I considered making an authentic-looking turtle shell out of some light stuffed material or bringing in a real turtle to let the kids watch it and follow it. But before I could turn these ideas into action, these little 4-year-olds got the idea of Big Turtle working beautifully. I think they just decided that it was time for the turtle to wake up and start moving.

Big Snake

Description

Did you ever see a little-people snake that wiggles and squiggles and hisses its way across the forest, jungle, or desert? If not, then you'd better let your children introduce you to Big Snake.

1. The children start in pairs by stretching out on their tummies, one child holding the ankles of the person in front of her to make a two-person snake that slithers across the floor on its belly.
2. They soon connect up to make a four-person snake, an eight-person snake, and so on, until the whole group is one big snake.
3. At various lengths, the children like to see if they can turn the whole snake over on its back without its coming apart. The snake can also go over "mountains," through "holes," or up "trees," or it may curl up and go to sleep. It takes a coordinated snake to do these feats. What children seem to enjoy most is getting the whole snake together.

Family of Elephants

Equipment

Optional: "elephants" made of a stick with a head and tail (see description), one for each pair of children

Description

In pairs, children create an elephant (or other animals) with their bodies or by both straddling a stick that has a head (e.g., decorated paper bag) and tail (rope) attached to it. Human arms make fine elephant trunks. Elephants plod or gallop around the room, connecting trunks (arms) to tails (ropes), until the whole family is linked together.

Variation

Secret messages, consisting of pictures of a certain number of elephants connected together or a certain number of horses doing something together, can be placed around the room. The children can share these picture messages with other elephants (or horses) and then all attempt to follow the picture (message).

Giant People and Animals

Description

Children play together to turn their bodies into different parts of a giant person or giant animal.

1. To begin, the children can suggest a specific animal or "giant" and propose its body parts. Each child can select a different body part.
2. The children then proceed to team up together with other children to make a total giant being.
3. Once they have their giant together, they can try to get it moving.
4. To add a fun challenge, once each group has formed its animal or giant, see if the children can get it to do specific tasks such as rolling over, curling up, stretching out, jumping, wagging its tail, and so on.

Variations

- Once children are familiar with this activity, they can simply be asked to make any kind of animal they want with two or more friends. They will make all sorts of things—horses, elephants, gorillas, even octopuses. On one occasion a horse transformed into an octopus right before my eyes, "so everyone could have a part." You never know precisely what the creation will look like, but everyone will be a part of it, and the children can tell you exactly what it is.

- Another cooperative option for making a collective person is for children to trace their own body parts on a long sheet of paper. This works well in groups of six. First, the children divide into pairs, each pair choosing one set of body parts (trunk and head, arms, legs). Each child then traces his partner's actual designated body part on a long piece of paper. They then help each other cut out the parts. Next the group puts all six body parts together on the floor, or on the wall using masking tape, to make one collective human being that they can color and decorate as they choose.

COOPERATIVE BODY GAMES

These are simple active games where children use their bodies to make the game work. Children enjoy the challenge of creating the game by working together with their bodies.

Wagon Wheels

Description

You need a fairly big play area and walls that are fairly free of obstacles to play this game, which is fun for children and adults alike. It doesn't sound like much when you read about it, but playing it takes you into another dimension.

1. To create the wagon wheel, about seven children face each other and join hands to make a circle.
2. The wheel then moves in a circular motion along the walls of the play area. Two or three children (the bottom of the wheel) have their backs touching the wall momentarily as the wheel spins along the wall. The fun increases as the wheel picks up speed. As a 6-year-old said to me, "It wheely works!"

Variation

Try putting the wheel in reverse or changing the speed limit for more fun. The wheel can also stop by turning itself into a human hubcap. To do this, one child lets go of her wheelmate's hand and begins to turn toward the inside of the circle, drawing the line into the center. This coiling process continues until everyone, still holding hands, is wrapped into a human hub. The children can then unwind and begin rolling again.

Spinning Star

Description

Young children enjoy playing this simple game.

1. Groups of about four children get together, and each child places his right hand in the center of the circle and holds onto the hand or wrist of another player.
2. They all face the same direction and walk around the circle to get the star moving.
3. To get the star spinning faster, the children walk quickly or jog around, still maintaining hand contact.
4. They then stop the star, face the other direction, and spin their star in the opposite direction.

Double Bubble

Description

"Bubbles" are formed by two or three children holding hands to make a small circle. The bubbles begin by floating around the room slowly, being careful not to bump into any other bubbles to avoid being popped. The objective of the game is for the children to work together to create their bubble and move their bubble around without any collisions. The bubbles can walk, hop, bop, or twirl around once the children become familiar with the game.

Variations

- To vary the game, circles of children in groups of two or three are still bubbles, but the objective becomes to merge the smaller bubbles into bigger bubbles. This can be done by two three-person bubbles gently squeezing together until the bubble pops into a six-person bubble. This process continues until there is only one giant bubble.
- Music can add extra fun to this game.

Human Bridges or Tunnels

Description

1. To play this game, half of the children make a human bridge with their arms, feet, or bodies, and the other half of the children crawl through the opening they have made.
2. To make a hand bridge, partners begin by making two lines facing each other. They then lean toward each other, grasp hands, and make a tunnel. This can be done on the knees to make a low tunnel.

3. To make a foot bridge, partners make two lines facing each other. They then lie down on their backs (or sit down) and raise their legs so the bottoms of their feet are supported by the bottoms of their partner's feet. This forms a low V-shaped tunnel.
4. Once the bridge is constructed, the other half of the children crawl through. Then they switch roles—the crawlers become bridge builders, and the bridge builders become crawlers.

Sticky Popcorn

Description

The children begin this game by "popping"—jumping or hopping—around the play area as individual pieces of sticky popcorn, searching for other pieces of popcorn. When one piece of popcorn comes into contact with another piece, they stick together. Once stuck, they continue to pop around together, sticking to other pieces, until they end up in several groups or in one big popcorn ball.

From our experience with 5-year-olds, be forewarned that sticky popcorn balls may begin to pop up at the strangest times—on the way down to the play area or while children are in the process of getting their coats off after playing outside.

Variation

Another popping option is for the children to "pop corn" in a group by forming a tightly knit circle with their arms around each other (or hand in hand). Several popping balls (from 3 to 23 soft soccer-sized balls) are placed inside the circle on the floor or ground, and the children move the circle as a unit from one point to another, trying to keep all the balls inside.

People Machine

Description

The only requirement for this game is an active imagination and a cooperative spirit.

1. Children begin by dividing into groups of four, six, or eight and pretend that they are all parts of a machine and must work together for the machine to run.
2. The children decide what kind of machine they create. It can be something real (e.g., a large robot or fire engine) or totally imaginary. What they create and how each of the children becomes a part of it is totally up to them.

3. The machine "turns on" when you give the "machine on" signal or start to play music. At that moment the machine starts to move its parts, which are the legs, heads, hands, arms, hips, and bodies of the players.
4. When you give the "machine off" signal or stop the music, the machine stops.

Variations

- If you need a little more structure to get started, all the children can hold hands and form a line, making a simple moving machine. Every other child can be asked to bend her trunk forward while the rest of the children bend their trunks backward, or to squat down when the others all stand up, or to raise their left legs up and down, and so on.
- The children can also pretend to be a smile-making machine or a laughing machine, with everyone smiling and laughing as they enter the machine. Older kids might enjoy making a more complicated machine, such as a human pinball machine.
- The children enjoy playing this laughing game while listening to "Laughing" on my audio CD *Changing Channels: Positive Living Skills for Children* (see Resources, page 160).

PARACHUTE AND BLANKET GAMES

There are some great cooperative games that you can play with children that involve the use of a blanket or parachute. These games will get you started, and with the help of your children, you can create many others.

Parachute

Equipment

One play parachute for each group of about 25 to 30 children

Description

A play parachute provides still another means of inflating the cooperative spirit.

1. The players spread themselves around the chute, grasping hold of its edge. Everyone then bends the knees (squats down to the floor or ground), and on the "up" signal the chute is inflated by everyone lifting the arms over head in unison. Once the chute is

inflated, the children can walk in beneath it toward the center (still holding on to the edges), meet in the center under the chute, and then walk back out to their original positions.

2. For the next game, each player standing around the chute is given a number from one to five. You can start with any child and count off, "1, 2, 3, 4, 5–1, 2, 3, 4, 5," as you point to the next child in the circle. Every child then has his own number between 1 and 5. Once they have a number, players stand around the chute holding it at waist level. In unison they bend their knees (squat down), and on the "up" signal all stand up and raise their hands over their heads (still holding onto the chute). When the chute is up in the air, one number (or group name) is called, and each member of that group lets go of the chute and walks under the chute to an open spot on the other side. This continues until all five groups have had a turn walking under the parachute.
3. For another game when a number is called, each member of that group goes under the chute and lies face up on the ground in the form of a star (like facedown skydivers linked together). The remaining players shake the chute up and down on them for about 15 to 20 seconds, giving them an air wave.
4. A good game to end with is to inflate the chute in the usual manner and in unison walk in beneath the chute toward the center. While the players are in the center under the inflated chute, they all let go of the chute at the same time and freeze in place. If they all let go *at the same time,* the chute will gently float back down on them. Players can learn to let go together by getting on their knees, holding the edge of the chute while it is on the floor (pulling it tight), and releasing it on the "let go" signal. If the chute is released at the same time, it will spring evenly toward the center.

Helpful Tips

- Parachute activities can begin with very young children and continue through virtually all age ranges. The parachute is a good medium for teaching children the value of cooperation. You cannot inflate a parachute yourself unless you are jumping out of a plane. The children have to work together to get the puffy results they want. For additional cooperative parachute activities, see *The Second Cooperative Sports and Games Book* in the Resources section.
- If you do not have the resources to buy a play parachute, you might be able to get an old parachute from a skydiving club, military outpost, or surplus store; or you might try sewing together a few sheets of light nylon or sails, leaving a hole in the middle (for air to get through).

Magic Carpet

Equipment

One sturdy blanket or extra-large and strong beach towel or gym mat (that will slide when pulled across the floor) for each group of about seven or eight children

Description

A group of about seven or eight children take turns giving each other magic-carpet rides on a gym mat or sturdy blanket. With kindergarten children, the middle person's "ride" can consist of getting jiggled around in one spot, which they all seem to enjoy. In some cases the "carpet" is pulled steadily to the other side of the room or gym, with the middle person lying, sitting, or crouching on the blanket or mat. The rider can choose a safe riding position and can control the speed ("Slower," "Faster," "Just right"). In the beginning, a rotation for taking turns could be suggested, or the rides can occur spontaneously, depending on the group. Five- and 6-year-olds also enjoy giving their favorite teddy bears, stuffed animals, or play people rides on the magic carpet.

Grasshopper in the Blanket

Equipment

One sturdy blanket or extra-large beach towel and one beach ball for each group of about 8 to 10 children

Description

The name of the game came from a 6-year-old girl who thought the ball definitely represented a grasshopper. See what you think. About 8 to 10 children arrange themselves standing around the edges of a sturdy blanket or large beach towel. A beach ball (grasshopper) is placed in the center of the blanket, and the children try to make it "hop." It usually takes 5-year-olds several sessions to get the hang (or hop) of this, particularly moving as a unit to catch the grasshopper, but they do get it. It's fun, and the grasshopper can do other things, too, such as rolling around the outside edge of the blanket, just missing everyone's fingers (where they hold on to the blanket).

Variations

- For added excitement and challenge, let the children bring in teddy bears or their favorite stuffed animals for the blanket toss.
- Put a balloon in the center of the blanket and tell the children it is a breakable egg. Thus, they have to move, cradle, and roll it very gently; otherwise, it will break. This one works well with preschoolers.
- Another option is to cut a hole in the center of the blanket, big enough for a soft, squishy ball or small beach ball or balloon to pass through. See if the kids can get the grasshopper to roll through the hole or jump into the air and come down through the hole.
- These activities work well with a small parachute, too.

Helpful Tip

Remind the children that it takes a cooperative effort to get that grasshopper high in the air and then back onto the blanket, without letting the grasshopper fall on the floor or ground. Assure them that they can do it if they work together.

ACTION GAMES

These are fun and active games that children really enjoy. Be prepared; if you play them once, the children will be asking to play them over and over again.

Fish Gobbler

Description

A big favorite! Five- and 6-year-old kids love this one. All you need is an area big enough for all the children to spread out with ample room to maneuver.

1. When the caller (also known as the fish gobbler) shouts, "Ship," all the children run toward the wall to which the caller points (wall number one).
2. When the caller shouts, "Shore," the children quickly change directions and run toward the opposite wall (wall number two).
3. On the signal "Fish gobbler," the children drop to the floor on their bellies and link arms, legs, or bodies together with one or more friends.
4. The fish gobbler moves around the room with arms outstretched like a big bird or manta ray swimming toward the other players but not touching any of them. The children are all "safe" as long as they are physically linked together with another child, or "fish."

5. Once the fish gobbler sees that everyone is linked to one or more partners, the signal "Rescue" is called. At this moment all the children jump to their feet, join hands, and yell, "Yay!" raising their joined hands over their heads. The game continues until the children are tired or are ready to move on to another game.

Variations

- Sardines: Everyone runs to a central point to make the tightest group possible by either lying on the floor or forming a massive standing hug.
- Jelly Belly Float: Everyone runs to wall number three, lies down on the floor, and pretends to be floating calmly and quietly like a jellyfish.
- Fishermen All: Everyone runs to wall number four, finds a partner, and sits back to back.
- Crabs: All the children back up to a partner, bend over, and reach under their own legs to hold hands.
- Treasure Island: Everyone runs to some treasure chests, finds something interesting (e.g., a little teddy bear), and gives it to another child—so everyone has a treasure.
- Fishnet: Let the kids use their imaginations and decide how to do one.

Helpful Tips

- When you introduce this game, start by using just two walls and a couple of simple calls. Later on you can use all four walls and add various other calls.
- This game can be easily adapted to theme days, such as teddy bear day or beach day, where children bring in a teddy bear or dress as if they are going to the beach.

Cooperative Trains

Description

The 5- and 6-year-olds never seem to tire of this one.

1. Children begin this game by forming two-person trains that chug around the gym, maintaining contact by keeping both hands on the hips (or shoulders) of the child immediately in front of them.
2. Ask the children to link together with other trains until there is one big train moving in unison.

3. The conductor (teacher or child) can see if the train can go up a steep hill really slowly, swoosh down the hill, go backward, get the cars really close together, make train noises, or bend down to go through a low tunnel. This very active cooperative game is lots of fun.

Helpful Tip

An interesting part of this game at all age levels is that when pairs of children begin trying to link up behind other pairs, they will eventually end up in a circle—even when some two-person trains are trying not to let other trains link up behind them.

Scooter Trains

Equipment

One gym scooter for each pair of children in the group (a gym scooter looks like a small plastic moving dolly with four wheels that allow it to move freely in any direction; the surface area of the scooter where the child sits measures about 12 by 12 inches, or 30 by 30 centimeters)

Description

We introduce this game first to 5- and 6-year-olds, but it can be lots of fun to play at any age level, including adults.

1. To begin the game, each pair of children is given one scooter.

2. One child sits on top of the scooter without his feet touching the floor. He holds on by placing his fingers through the handhold slots on each side of the scooter. Tell the children to place their fingers inside the slots rather than outside to protect them from getting bumped.
3. The partner who is not sitting on the scooter stands behind the scooter, places both her hands on the other child's back, and guides him around the gym.
4. On the "change positions" signal, the children switch positions so that each child gets a chance to ride and guide.

Variations

- After each partner has learned the basics of how to maneuver safely around the gym, you can introduce other more challenging options. For example, set up a slalom course with marker cones, and ask the children if they can safely guide each other through the obstacle course without hitting any obstacles and without anyone falling off. You can start this game by asking pairs of children to line up in front of the obstacle course, then send them down the course one set of partners at a time, leaving some space between them. When each set of partners gets to the end of the course, the children can wheel back to the beginning of the course and switch positions for the next run through the course.
- For larger challenges and more cooperation, ask the children if they can link the scooters together to make a very large scooter car or bus or train or ambulance or limo. Suggest that some children might want to link together sitting on their scooters while other children help them move along by standing on the side next to them to guide the train in the direction they want to go. Players can then switch positions so the riders become guiders. With one kindergarten class, we asked all the boys to sit on their scooters to make a scooter train. We asked all the girls to help them link together, help them stay on their scooters, and guide their train around the room. They were successful, and there were cheers all around. Then they switched roles: the girls formed the scooter train, and the boys did the guiding. This also worked well, and again there were cheers all around. Children can create many different options for playing this game—set the guideline of cooperation and fun for everyone, then see what they come up with.

Helpful Tip

Before starting, talk with the children about how to play this game in a safe and respectful way. It is best to start slowly, then gradually increase speed and gradually slow down. The guiding goal is for all partners to move safely around the gym at the same time, with lots of smiles and no bumps or crashes. Each child is responsible for taking care of not only her partner but also all other players scooting around the play area.

Cooperative Musical Hugs

Equipment

A stereo and CD or other way of playing music

Description

The kids call it Hugs, and it's an active way to start a cooperative play session.

1. Play energizing music or sing an uplifting song while the children skip around the room or play area.
2. When you stop the music, each child quickly teams up with someone else in a hug.
3. The kids skip around again (with partners if they want) when the music continues.
4. The next time the music stops, at least three kids hug together. As the game goes on, they make a bigger and bigger hug, until finally all the children squish together in one massive musical hug. This is a wonderful way to bring young children closer together in an active, feel-good way.

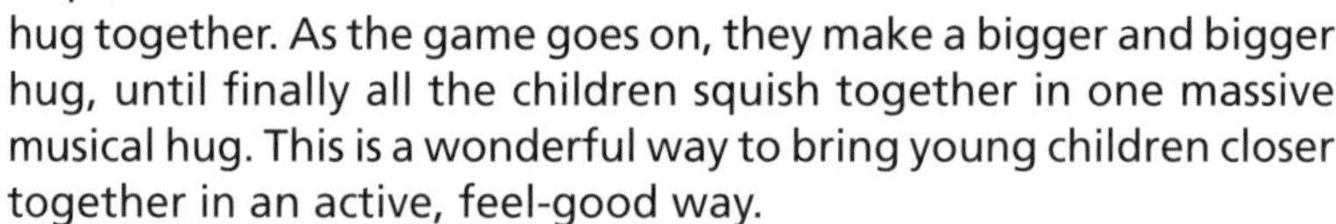

QUIET GAMES

It is nice to have a mix of active and quiet games. The children enjoy their cooperative quiet games, and it is a great way to slow things down and create a sense of calm and tranquility.

Secret Message

Description

Secret messages still have great intrigue for 5-year-olds (and I would venture to say for people of all ages). In this game, all the children sit close together in a tight circle and pass whispers to their friends.

1. A parent, teacher, or child selects a word or short phrase (e.g., "I like you") and whispers it into the ear of the person on the right.
2. The secret is passed on to the next person until everyone has received the message.
3. The last person then says the message out loud, and the children compare it with the original secret message.

Variations

- To add challenge and fun, messages can be passed around faster and faster, or the same phrase (or different phrases) can be started around the circle in both directions.
- The children can also pass friendly silent messages or "signs," such as a happy smile, a warm hug, a gentle squeeze, a handshake, raised eyebrows, or a wink.

Helpful Tip

This fun, quiet game requires good listening and focusing skills. Remind the children to listen closely and to focus on hearing and feeling the secret message. It's amazing how even 5-year-olds are attentive and curious to hear how the message will "turn out."

Puzzles

Equipment

Puzzle pieces made from old magazines, posters, or the children's drawings

Description

A simple and effective way to pair people up or link many people together, where everyone is important and no one feels left out, is through the use of puzzles. For pairs, cut some magazine pictures in half, hand them out, and ask the children to find the other half of their puzzle. For larger groups (e.g., six to eight children), glue some posters on poster boards; or let the children draw their own pictures, cut them into the appropriate number of pieces, hand them out, and let the children find the people who complete their puzzle. This linking-up process is particularly helpful in cases where some children are shy or not normally chosen as partners or teammates by other children.

Shapes

Description

The children play this game in teams of two, three, four, or more, depending on the challenge presented. Start with three or four children in a group. Ask them if they can make a certain number (e.g., one, two, three, four), shape (e.g., circle, triangle, square), or letter with their bodies. How they do it is up to them, just as long as everyone in the group is a part of it. If they feel they need more partners, different groups can team together to meet the challenge. On one occasion, a group of eight 4-year-olds made a "circle" with their heads; 5- and 6-year-olds made beautiful threes with their three bodies; and four 7-year-olds made cool *X*s and even double *X*s.

Variations

- Older children can join together to spell words (e.g., their names) with their bodies, or the whole class can spell a "body sentence."
- This game of meaningful connection can also be played outdoors or even in shallow water with various age groups. The children will usually find their own way to make it work.

Helpful Tip

Three or four little minds can work well together with their little bodies to form numbers, shapes, and some animals. For most challenges, the children themselves can come up with the number of bodies they need for their unique approach and find a way to make sure everyone is included—which is a requirement for a successful outcome.

Tug of Peace: Rope Shapes

Equipment

One skipping rope or similar length of rope for each group of three children

Description

Contrary to Tug of War, where teams pull against each other, Tug of Peace allows all children holding a single rope to cooperate to meet the final objective. All you need is some rope or skipping ropes and some children focused on cooperating.

1. The children divide into groups and attempt to create specific patterns using a rope. For example, to make a rope triangle, three children (or more) need to work together to pull gently to keep the rope taut at specific points.
2. Different letters and shapes can be introduced that require more points or bends in the rope, which in turn encourages larger group interaction and more cooperation.

Variations

- Different groups can join together to make more complicated patterns. Eventually all the ropes can be joined together, and the whole class can work as a cooperative team to make the shapes.
- To make this game more physically active, the children can run to designated points before making the shape and then running back to their starting point. In this case, all team members maintain contact with the rope during the run (maintaining the shape, throwing the rope over their shoulders, circling it around them, or whatever they decide).

Helpful Tip

A challenging part of this game for some groups may lie in overcoming the concept of "tug of war." If some children begin to pull too hard, it is a great opportunity to remind them to redirect their energy toward achieving the goal together. This is the way to win this game.

Shoe Twister

Equipment

One pair of shoes, slippers, or sandals for each child (whatever they are wearing on their feet will work fine)

Description

1. Each child removes one indoor shoe and places it in a pile.
2. Everyone then picks up someone else's shoe from the pile. While holding the shoe (method left up to the children's ingenuity—each child can decide how she will hold the shoe or they can all decide at the beginning how everyone will hold the shoes), everyone joins hands or links arms, forming a large circle.
3. Each child then locates the owner of the shoe she is holding by carefully looking at the shoe every other child is still wearing.

4. All children then try to give the shoe they are holding to its rightful owner by exchanging shoes without breaking their joined hands or linked arms. This process tends to unfold in waves of exchanges in order to not break the circle. For younger children, directions can be given to help them solve the challenge; older children can figure it out on their own. Groups of younger children can use their hands. Once all shoes have been returned to their owners, the circle is reformed, and children make another pile of shoes to start the game again.

Positive Yarn

Equipment

One ball of thick yarn or strips of old sheets tied together at the ends and rolled up into a ball

Description

This is an interesting way to knit young children together.

1. One child starts with a bright ball of thick yarn (or a long strip of material rolled into a ball), wraps the end of the yarn around her waist, and passes the ball to another child.
2. As she passes the ball to the next child, she says one nice thing to that child—something that will make him feel good.
3. He wraps the yarn around his waist and passes it to another child as he says one nice thing to that person, and so on. Once the whole group (or a group of about eight players) has been intertwined in positive yarn, the process is reversed. The last player begins to slowly rewind the ball, passes it to the next child, says something positive to that child, and so on until the fully wound ball reaches the first child.

Variation

You can also use different colors of yarn to link people together. In this game, children sit in a circle and make links in the following way. "If you know a person's name, take a red piece of yarn and stretch it out between where you are sitting and where that person is sitting." (To do this the child picks up the red ball of yarn, rolls it toward the other person, and cuts the piece of yarn with a pair of scissors; that piece of yarn stays on the floor, linking those two children. Then that child goes back to the spot where he was sitting.) "If you played with someone at recess, take a green piece of yarn and stretch it out between you and that child." "If you know where someone lives or you played at his house, take a yellow piece of yarn and stretch it out between you and that person." "If you like a person, or if a person did something nice for you or said something nice to you, take a blue piece of yarn and stretch it out between you and that person."

Helpful Tip

This game can go in lots of directions and lead to some positive interaction about how to be nice on other children's feelings. Remember to include everyone, and try to find ways to make all children feel connected or valued in some way.

Tiptoe Through the Tulips

Equipment

A long sheet of white, brown, or colored construction paper; bowls of three or four different watercolor paints; some paint brushes

Description

The children work together to create a lovely lane of tulips through which they can tiptoe.

1. First the children paint a long, winding lane of flowers and leaves—and if they like, also paint one another's toes—with the brightly colored paints.
2. Then the real fun begins—tiptoeing through the tulips. How they tiptoe is left totally to their own imaginations and is sure to elicit some smiles all around.
3. Once the collective creation is completed, the children hang the mural together.

Helpful Tip

This activity can get a little messy. You might want to play this game on a surface that is easy to clean or outside on a bright spring day, with singing and music—and a bucket or hose to wash off, too.

UNIQUE COOPERATIVE GAMES

There are some unique cooperative games in this section including a potato sack designed for a group of people (as opposed to a potato sack race) and ideas for finishing activities together at the same time.

Little People's Big Sack

Equipment

One big sack (e.g., a large potato sack) that the whole group can climb into or several smaller sacks that will hold about seven people

Description

We have made several different-sized big sacks that hold between 8 and 20 children. They climb into the sack and try to maneuver it by collective shuffling, hopping, crawling, or rolling. The first sack we made came from an old burlap canoe cover. We simply cut it up and sewed it together in the shape of a giant potato sack. The second one we made out of durable old white sheets, and the most recent one was a cover for a comforter or duvet which already had a slip or opening at one end. In both cases the sacks were light, and the kids could see through the material, which guarded against anyone feeling too closed in.

One kindergarten teacher commented on how Big Sack was increasingly well received at different points in her cooperative games program:

> First time: "What a delight! Half of them in the bag [big sack] trying to roll from the back of the room to the front of the room. Many squeals of delight from inside the bag. The half left out fought over who was getting in next . . . rotten crew! Mad when it was put away."

Later in program: "Today I just put the bag on the floor and said nothing. Most of them [16] got in but didn't fit well (they couldn't move as a unit). Tina [5-year-old girl] organized the entire group—to get in one at a time and get closer together. 'If we work together, it's for sure going to work,' she said. It did, with only one difference of opinion."

Still later in the program: "Big sack outside on the grass—what fun! The more it's used, it appears the better they get along. There were no overt nasties."

Rescue

Equipment

Some simple objects that can be used as part of an obstacle course (hula hoop, bench, rubber door mat, duct tape on the floor)

Description

With practice, this game nurtures positive communication, empathy, and trust between children. One kindergarten teacher commented, "My children love this game and have real empathy for the 'blind' person. Once the stage is set, they demonstrate a gentleness that I don't see in other games."

1. Two children are lost in a snowstorm (or sandstorm) and are trying to get back home. One of the children is "snow-blind," but the other can see. The objective is to lead the snow-blind friend (who has his eyes shut or is blindfolded) through the storm (obstacle course) to safety.
2. In pairs, the children go through a snow tunnel (hoop), under an ice log (bench), over a partially frozen river (small mat or strips of duct tape), and across a snow bridge (bench). Partners try to remain in contact by holding hands or linking arms throughout the journey "so no one gets lost alone in the storm." Once they reach "safety," the partners can switch roles.

Variations

- For kids who have never experienced a snowstorm or sandstorm, the story can be changed to something like "control tower to pilot." The pilot cannot see because of heavy fog. The objective is for the controller to direct the pilot safely through various obstacles and onto the runway.
- For additional challenge (or older groups), the children can attempt to direct a partner through the course safely only by talking to

her, by singing to her, or by using a special code (e.g., clap hands to move one way; tap shoulder to step up; or snap finger, hum, or use a musical instrument for special instructions). Children can lead a partner around appropriately challenging obstacles (indoors or outdoors) or through a designated task using a code the two have devised, with or without speaking.

Helpful Tip

Children with visual impairments could be included in this game both as the guider and the one being guided. If there are "markers" for them to feel along the way—like duct tape on the floor at various points showing the direction of the course—the challenge will likely be appropriate for them.

What Can You Do Together?

Description

This game has an infinite number of variations. The common thread running through the different activities is that children are challenged to achieve the objective by performing the task together or by acting out the motions or emotions with one or more friends.

Can you walk through a field of sticky glue with your partner?

Can you swim through Jell-O with your partner?

Can you be really tall with your partner?

Can you be really small with your partner?

Can you be one frog with your partner?

Can you be a round thing with your friend while holding her hand?

Can you pretend to bounce your partner like a ball?

Can you and your partner hold hands and saw wood together like lumberjacks?

Can you make a human chair for your partner to sit on?

Can you make a two-person chair?

A four-person chair?

Can you skip around with three friends?

Can you get behind your partner, wrap your arms around his front, and walk at the same time as he does?

Can four people do it?

Can you make a fort with your friends and all get inside it?

Can you go through an obstacle course (e.g., under a bench, through a hoop, across a beam) without letting go of your partner's hand?

Can you make a people tunnel that someone can go through? Can you take turns going through the tunnel but keep the tunnel as long as possible?

Can you find your partner's heartbeat? After a quiet game? After an active game?

Can you be very quiet and relax with your partner?

Can you each get a stick (or broom) and together try to bounce and catch a beach ball using both your sticks?

Can you get in groups of three or four and see if you can carry a beach ball across the room, holding it way over your heads with floor-hockey sticks or brooms?

With your back stuck to your partner's back, can you move around the room? Jump forward toward this wall? Jump backward toward this wall? Both get inside a hoop and move around, still stuck back to back?

Can you roll a big hula hoop on its edge so your partner can run through it?

Can your partner roll it so you can run through it?

Can you make a people sandwich with four or five friends? (e.g., with ham, lettuce, mustard, and two slices of bread)

Can you sit down across from your friend, feet to feet, and row a boat?

Can you roll your partners like a log? Can you jump over your logs? Can you (and a friend) drag your logs across the floor? Can you (and a friend) stand your log up like a telephone pole?

Can you share a highlight (or something you had fun doing) with your partner?

Can you and your partner act out a highlight (or something you had a lot of fun doing) so that two other friends can guess what it is from your actions?

Can you think of some other cool activities to try to do together?

Exactly the Same Time

Description

In this game, children of all ages are challenged to see if they can do something or finish doing something at exactly the same time. The task may be very simple, but finishing at the same moment can be very challenging.

Can you and your partner start spinning a bottle, top, or coin at the same moment and have them stop at the same time?

Can you both start eating a carrot or apple at the same time and finish at the same moment?

Can you walk at the same time, same stride, same pace, and finish at exactly the same time?

Can you talk at the same time and finish at the same moment?

Can you start making the same sandwich at the same time and finish at exactly the same time?

Can you start getting dressed and finish at exactly the same time?

Can you think of some fun activities or interesting tasks to try to do at exactly the same time?

When you try to do something at exactly the same time as your friend or partner, you begin to discover what it takes to do it successfully. It both requires and helps develop a keen sense of awareness of the other person, an element of empathy, good anticipation skills, and lots of cooperation.

COOPERATIVE GYMNASTICS

A great number of gymnastics stunts can be executed only with one or more partners (e.g., pyramids, double rolls, foot pitches, teeterboard stunts, even the flying trapeze). Consult a good gymnastics book (such as Peter Werner's *Teaching Children Gymnastics, Second Edition*, Human Kinetics, 2004) on stunts and tumbling for a wide selection to choose from. A few simple cooperative stunts for young children are presented here.

Partner Pull-Up

Description

1. Partners sit down facing each other with the soles of their feet on the floor, toes touching.
2. Partners reach forward, bending their knees if they must, and grasp hands.
3. By pulling together, both partners stand up and then try to slowly return to a sitting position.

Variation

Partner Pull-Up can also be done in groups of three, four, five, or more.

Partner Back-Up

Description

1. Two children sit back to back, knees bent, with the bottoms of their feet flat on the floor.
2. From this position, they try to stand up by pushing against each other's backs without moving their feet.
3. Sitting down again slowly can also be attempted. If the children are successful at sitting down again, propose that from a halfway position they try to move like a spider.

Variation

Partner Back-Up can be done in groups of three, four, or five.

Long Log Roll

Description

Partners lie flat on their backs—head to head—with arms stretched straight out above their heads on the floor. They grasp hands or wrists. Partners then try to roll across the floor like a log while keeping hand contact.

Variation

For additional challenge, players can add more partners to make a longer log roll. The first two children remain stretched out on the floor. Two other children link to their feet by lying on the floor and holding onto their ankles with their hands. They then all work together to get their four-people-long log rolling.

Wring the Dishrag

Description

1. Two children stand facing each other and join right hands (as if shaking hands).
2. Player 1 lifts his right leg over the head of player 2 as she bends down or squats, so player 1 ends up in a straddle position over his own arm.
3. Player 2 lifts her left leg over player 1 in the same manner. The partners are now back to back (actually, behind to behind).
4. Player 1 continues by bringing his left leg over the head of player 2 and facing the original direction. Player 2 lifts her right leg over the head of player 1 to the original face-to-face position.

Helpful Tip

I know it sounds complicated, and you might be shaking your head trying to visualize doing it, but it's actually simple. Grab someone right now and try it . . . you'll see.

Hop-Along

Description

1. Partners stand facing each other. Both raise the left leg straight out, just high enough for each partner to grasp hold of the other person's ankle.
2. Once they can balance each other in this position, partners can try to hop along (to the market, to the store) or may even try to lower themselves down to the floor. Coming back up is a little tougher and may require the help of a few more friends.

Tug of Peace: Rope Pull-Up

Equipment

One piece of rope about the length of a skipping rope for each group of three or four children

Description

In this game, the ends of the rope or ropes are tied together, and children work together to pull each other up off the floor. For example, children make a rope triangle or a rope square, and while outside the rope facing each other in a seated position, they all pull hard (but not too hard) so they can all come up to a standing position.

Variation

A longer and thicker climbing rope tied in a circle can let various age groups feel the power of people pulling together. First place the rope in a circle on the floor or grass. The participants begin by sitting down outside the rope, facing the center of the circle. Each player then grasps the rope with both hands, and they all pull together so that everyone rises to their feet, still holding the rope. They can then slowly lower themselves back down to a seated position.

With adult groups, some participants stand on the rope, with their hands secure on the shoulders of two pullers. When the whole group pulls together, those standing on the rope easily rise into the air. In the end, all the pullers are standing on the ground with the rope at waist level, all the standers are standing on the rope, and everyone is feeling and admiring the power of the whole group.

Toesie Roll

Description

If you are going to have cooperative heads, you might just as well have cooperative feet. Kindergarten and first-grade children giggle all the way through this one. Partners simply lie stretched out on the floor, feet to feet (or big toe to big toe), and attempt to roll across the floor keeping their toes touching throughout. Toesie Roll can also be attempted with only the toes of the right feet connected; with legs crisscrossed; or while in a sitting (L) position, rolling toe to toe. Try it!

Cooperative Cycling

Description

1. Partners lie stretched out on the floor, feet to feet. They need to get close enough to each other so that the bottoms of their feet stay connected while lying on their backs with their feet in a bicycling position.

2. They start out pedaling slowly with their feet glued together (by the pressure of feet pressing on feet). They try to cycle faster and faster and then slow down and stop before cycling their legs in the opposite direction. Only their legs are actually moving. Co-op cyclers usually lie flat on their backs, but they can also try a partially seated V position, with hands or elbows behind them supporting their upper bodies. This is a good activity for any age level.

Variations

- For added fun and challenge, try co-op three-way cycling with three people—six feet pedaling at the same time. To do this, start lying on the ground, with each person placing the bottom of one foot on the bottom of the person's foot on each side of them.
- Partners can also try co-op arm cycling while facing each other in a standing, seated, or kneeling position.

COOPERATIVE BALANCING ACTIVITIES

Cooperative balancing activities are a good way to get children working together toward a common goal. When engaged in most of these activities, children quickly realize that if they work together, there is a good chance they will be successful in executing the task; equally important, if they do not cooperate, their team will not succeed.

Tray Balance

Equipment

One cafeteria tray or piece of thin wooden or plastic board a little larger than a cafeteria tray, one block of wood or plastic, and one ball for each set of partners

Description

This introductory balancing activity gives children a successful experience with partner balancing.

1. Each pair of children is given a board or cafeteria tray with a block on it. Each child holds one end of the tray, and together they walk across the room, one walking forward and the other backward or both walking sideways.
2. The children attempt to move in different directions without bumping into anyone or anything and without dropping the block. To increase the challenge, ask them to balance a ball on the tray while walking, running, or jumping around the play area.

Variation

Tray Balance on Bench: The two children try to balance the block or ball while walking across a wide board, a sturdy bench, a tree trunk, or a very low balance beam, depending on their capabilities. Instruct the children to take responsibility for the other person by indicating when she is approaching the end of the bench—the other child can then prepare to step down safely.

Wand Balance

Equipment

Three bamboo sticks, plastic wands, or similar objects and one ball for each pair of children

Description

1. Pairs of children are given two long bamboo sticks or plastic wands, which they hold as if they were holding a stretcher. Place a third stick or wand across the other two.
2. The children attempt to walk across the floor or a bench or beam without letting the third wand fall off. A ball can also be placed on the two wands or sticks for additional challenge.

Object Balance

Equipment

One lightweight, unbreakable object for each pair of children

Description

1. Two children put a pillow, balloon, ball, or other lightweight, unbreakable object between their heads or bodies.
2. Then, without touching the object with their hands, they attempt to walk across the floor or a bench or beam. The children hold the object between them with the mutually applied support. To be done successfully, this activity involves close, continuous awareness of the partner and his movements. If partners do not move in a cooperative, synchronized manner, either the object will fall or one child will nudge the other off balance.

Joy's Inclination

Equipment

Two long benches or wood planks about the size of a bench

Description

1. Prop two parallel benches or planks of wood securely against a jungle gym or stall bars so that they are slightly inclined.
2. Ask the children to walk forward and then backward on the sloping bench, with a partner on the floor holding them by the hand and spotting them in case they lose their balance.
3. Two children then hold hands and walk side by side on top of the two sloping benches, first forward up the plank and then backward down the plank. They then turn and face each other and sidestep up and down the benches, holding hands.

Variations

- For very balanced children, the side step can be repeated, with the children balancing a ball between two sticks while traveling up and down the benches.
- For additional challenge and cooperation, two children can begin by standing at opposite ends of the same bench. They walk toward each other, meet at the center of the bench, and try to develop a cooperative method to pass each other so that each child can continue to the other end. If they are successful at doing this on a flat bench on the floor, some children might want to try it on a slightly inclined bench.

Balancing Bridges

Equipment

One plastic hockey stick or similar-sized object and one beanbag for each pair of children; benches, logs, or other objects to act as bridges

Description

This is a balancing act that requires the cooperation of two children to successfully complete the mission.

1. Children pair up and work together with one plastic hockey stick (or similar object) and a beanbag. Each child takes one end of the stick, and the two partners try to balance their beanbag in the middle of the stick while they move around the play area.
2. Generally the children face each other and begin by following the lines on the floor, which lead them to the various bridges (sturdy wooden benches lined up around the play area; logs in outdoor settings). As they climb up onto the first bridge, they try to keep the stick level and the beanbag in balance.
3. As they approach the end of the bench, the person walking forward tells his partner (who is walking backward) that the end of the bench is coming. ("Be careful . . . get ready . . . step down.") This is a good opportunity to nurture a concern for others' welfare.

Helpful Tip

Building balance and personal bridges is the ultimate goal.

SINGING GAMES

Cooperative songs can be used for more game-playing fun. Here are a few singing games we've enjoyed playing, but you can adapt the lyrics to songs your children know. In the latter three cooperative singing games, there is only intermittent active involvement. However, the kids like them, and that is a crucial test. Many children's games can be enhanced with the help of songs, music, dance, imagination, and cooperation among all participants. The four singing games presented here are just a start. See what you can find or create.

The More We Get Together

Description

The children begin the game by skipping around the gym, hand in hand, with one or two partners, singing:

The more we get together,
Together, together.
The more we get together,
The happier we'll be.
For your friends are my friends,
And my friends are your friends;
The more we get together,
The happier we'll be.

Every time they sing "together," more friends join together, until everyone is holding hands. At the end of the song, all the children form a circle and rush to the middle of the circle, raising their hands way up in the air and cheering.

The Big Ship Sails

Description

All the children hold hands and form a circle. Two children are chosen to start as the "ship," one holding on to the other's waist from behind. The children in the circle raise their arms, and the ship begins weaving in and out of the circle by repeatedly going under the raised arms of the other children as they all sing this song:

Oh, the big ship sails through
The alley alley o, the alley alley o,
The alley alley o.
Oh, the big ship sails through
The alley alley o,
Heigh ho alley alley o.

When the verse stops after "Heigh ho alley alley o," the ship also stops, and the two children with arms raised closest to the end of the ship join on to the back of the ship. The smaller circle reconnects, and the bigger ship weaves in and out again as the children sing the song. The ship continues to get bigger in this manner until finally all children are part of the big ship. They then sail around the room taking short, snappy steps and singing.

Thread the Needle

Description

About eight children join hands to form a line. The first child is the needle and begins by leading the line (thread) under the raised arms of the last two children (seventh and eighth), singing:

The thread follows the needle,
The thread follows the needle.
In and out the needle goes
As we mend the clothes.

The seventh child ends up facing the eighth with his arms crossed in front of him. This forms the first stitch. The needle then continues in the same direction and leads the line under the arms of the sixth and seventh children, which forms another stitch. This is repeated until the entire line has been stitched, with the leader turning under her own arm to complete the last stitch. To "rip" the stitch, the children raise their arms overhead, still holding hands, and turn back to their original positions. The eighth child now moves to the front of the line to become the new needle. Continue until everyone has had a turn as needle.

Here We Come Walking

Description

The children join hands, form a circle large enough for children to skip around inside, and sit down. To the first verse of the song, several children begin by walking hand in hand down the imaginary street inside the circle. On the second verse, they release their handhold to go and knock at a friend's imaginary door (tap on floor in front of a friend). Each child helps the new friend up by taking his hand, and all players in the middle of the circle join hands and skip around to the third verse. This procedure continues until everyone has come out to play; the number doubles each time they go knocking at the doors.

Here we come walking
Down the street, down the street.
Here we come walking down the street.
How are you today?

Here we come knocking
At your door, at your door.
Here we come knocking at your door.
Come outside and play.
La la la la la,
La la la, la la la,
La la la la la la la la,
La la la la la.

COOPERATIVE MATH AND SPELLING GAMES

The following games are designed to put a little more action, fun, and cooperation into math and spelling challenges. The same cooperative concepts can be applied to active learning in many different domains.

Line Up by Numbers

Equipment

A series of numbered cards, each card containing a number from 1 to 12

Description

This game is for younger children who are just getting to know their numbers. Place a series of numbered cards at the end of the room (for younger children, use numbers 1 to 10 or 12). Each child runs down and picks up one number. The children then work together to arrange themselves in numerical order, starting with 1 and ending with 12.

Variation

Children can also play this same game by running to pick up a letter in the alphabet and working together to line up in alphabetical order.

Sum Games

Equipment

A box of 40 to 50 beanbags; small sticks or any other object that is easy to carry; a blackboard for all groups or a flip chart and marker for each group

Description

1. Place a pile of beanbags at one end of the room. The children stand in groups of four at the opposite end of the play area.

2. Call out a number (e.g., seven). Each group of children runs to the beanbags. The children determine on their own how many bags each must pick up to equal the number that was called. Each child must carry at least one beanbag.
3. Once the children have the appropriate number of bags, they all run back to the other end of the gym. Each child records the number of bags he has picked up, stepping up on a bench (if necessary) to reach the blackboard or flip chart. The children then indicate the correct sign for addition and work together to add it up. The complexity of the task can be adapted for different groups.

Target Toss

Equipment

One cardboard target a bit larger than a dartboard and five balls or beanbags for each pair of children; a blackboard to write on

Description

1. Cardboard targets with an inner circle and an outer circle (like a big dart board) are placed at various points on the wall, one for every two children. The children work in pairs, one throwing and the other retrieving thrown balls.
2. The pitcher takes five throws at the target. If she hits the wall or floor, she gets one point; if she hits the large outside circle on the target, she gets two points; and if she hits the smaller inside circle, she gets three points.
3. Each child keeps a mental record of her own score. After five throws each, the children run to a blackboard and write down their scores. Partners work together to add up both of their scores.

Variation

At certain age levels, all pairs of children can work together to add up the entire group score. They can then return to the target area and attempt to increase their collective score.

Pot of Gold

Equipment

One cardboard box and about 40 beanbags (or any object that can be easily counted) for each team

Description

This running game incorporates the concepts of subtraction and sharing.

1. Place several pots (or cardboard boxes) containing "bags of gold" at one end of the room or gym, one pot of gold for each team.
2. The children count how many bags of gold are in their pot.
3. The children then decide on an object they would like to "buy" (e.g., a shovel or cake), and the storekeeper (parent or teacher) tells them the cost (in number of beanbags). Together, the small groups of children run to their pot and pull out the gold necessary. Each child must take at least one piece of gold.
4. Through subtraction they must then determine how much gold is remaining in their pot. When they think they know how much gold is remaining, they run to the other end of the gym to tell the storekeeper. When they are correct, they return the gold to their pot and begin a new game by selecting another item to buy.

Spelling Ball

Equipment

One ball for each pair of children

Description

The children divide into pairs, each pair sharing a ball. The pairs then attempt to go through the letters in the alphabet as they pass the ball back and forth. As a child passes the ball to his partner, he calls out the next letter. If one child is unsure of the next letter, his partner can give him a hint by drawing the shape of the letter with her finger on the floor or on her partner's back.

Variations

- Follow the same procedure to spell each other's names, animal names, colors, and so on.
- Vary the difficulty level of the words, the type of ball being passed, and the kinds of passes used to make them appropriate for the age level.

Spelling Volley

Equipment

A balloon or beach ball; a volleyball net

Description

Two teams, one on either side of a net, play a volleyball-type spelling game with a balloon or beach ball, depending on their skill level.

1. The two teams first decide on a word to spell.
2. When the ball is hit over the net, the team that hit the ball quickly forms the first letter with all their bodies (usually on the floor).
3. When the ball is bumped back over the net, the whole team on the other side forms the second letter, and so on until the word is completed.
4. The teams on the receiving side of the net can either catch the ball while the other team is forming the letter or keep the ball in play, depending on skill level.

Spell Sport

Equipment

Two or three sets of alphabet cards for each team

Description

1. Children divide into teams of about five or six and line up at one end of the room.
2. Scatter the lettered cards, including a period and exclamation mark, at the far end of the room.
3. Call out the name of a different sport to each group, or give clues about the different words to be spelled (e.g., played on a mat, two people involved, contact sport, nine-letter word. Get it? Wrestling!).
4. Each team then has one minute to work out a strategy before the "go" signal is given to run to the letters.
5. Each player must pick up or be touching at least one letter when the team returns to the starting line and spells the word by lining up in the proper order, with each player holding up a letter or letters.

Variation

Another option that ensures cooperation among all participants is to give the various teams different words that can be put together to spell a sentence. Words can be adapted to the age level and size of the group. Certain players may need to pick up more than one card, and occasionally two or more players may have to share, but every player must be in contact with at least one card when a team spells a sentence.

What's the Action?

Equipment

Two or three sets of alphabet cards for each team

Description

This game is played in a manner similar to Spell Sport.

1. Divide the children into small groups of about four or five.
2. The children watch as a teacher, leader, or child demonstrates an action (jump, skip, roll, spin, laugh, smile, wink, hug).
3. The children then think of a word that fits the action, locate the letters required to spell the word from a group of alphabet cards spread out on the floor, and work together to put the letters in the proper order (or write the word on the blackboard), with each child in the group being responsible for or sharing at least one letter.
4. The whole group then moves around the room together, acting out what the word says. The only rule is that the action must be something positive or nothing that would make anyone else feel bad.

Underwater Spelling

Equipment

Writing board that will work under water

Description

A team decides on a word, and each individual becomes responsible for writing a specific letter. The players then either write their word on an underwater writing board at the bottom of a large washing basin (where only the arm is submerged) or go to the bottom of a shallow pool and write the letters on a submerged writing board.

Helpful Tip

In all of our spelling games, words or sentences can be introduced that represent themes of cooperation, joy, and friendship.

GAMES FOR RELAXATION AND STRESS CONTROL

When children play cooperative games or are engaged in other joyful activities that make them feel totally accepted, valued, and fully included, a lot of the stress in their lives is reduced or eliminated. Engaging in activities that are joyful and uplifting in any context frees children (and adults)—at least temporarily—from stress, doubts, and worries. Experiences that energize children in positive ways make them more resilient to the negative effects of stress. Sharing highlights and participating in games of inclusion have a way of putting everything into a more positive perspective. If children are also equipped with a number of specific skills for relaxing themselves and managing the stress in their lives, they will be in a much better position to cope more effectively with stress and live with a higher sense of balance and harmony.

Games that teach children how to relax and control stress can be of great value because children can use these skills in a variety of situations for the rest of their lives. Relaxation games focus on teaching children how to cooperate with their own minds and bodies. Participants learn how to talk to their bodies and connect with their muscles and their breathing to calm down and relax. Following are two of my favorite games to encourage relaxation.

Learning to relax is as important as living an active lifestyle.

Spaghetti Toes

Equipment

Audio CD player and audio CD *Spaghetti Toes: Positive Living Skills for Children* (see Resources, page 160)

Description

In this activity, children pretend or imagine that different parts of their bodies are like cooked spaghetti lying on a plate. Children begin by lying down on the floor or by relaxing in chairs. Ask them to do the following: "Wiggle your toes. Stop wiggling your toes. Let your toes go soft and warm and sleepy like warm, cooked spaghetti lying on your plate. Now wiggle your legs. Stop wiggling your legs. Let your legs go soft and warm and sleepy like warm, cooked spaghetti lying on your plate." This same relaxation sequence is repeated to wiggle and then relax their hands, arms, shoulders, and so on until their entire bodies are completely relaxed.

Jelly Belly

Equipment

Audio CD player and audio CD *Spaghetti Toes: Positive Living Skills for Children* (see Resources, page 160)

Description

In this activity, children lie on the ground and place one hand on top of their belly buttons. Ask them to do the following: "Get yourself into a comfortable position. Breathe in easily and slowly, and try to make the hand on your belly go up. Breathe out slowly, and try to make the hand on your belly go down. Breathe in slowly—belly up. Breathe out slowly—belly down." They continue breathing in and out in this way until they are calm and relaxed. This is an effective way of teaching young children diaphragm breathing, or belly breathing, which can be used for quick relaxation in a number of different stressful situations. If you are interested in getting complete scripts and a series of audio CD activities for teaching young children to relax and control their stress, see my book *Feeling Great: Teaching Children to Excel at Living,* and consult the positive living skills audio CDs in the resource section at the end of this book.

CLEANING UP TOGETHER

Getting children to work together to clean up toys or play equipment at school, home, or in the gym or activity area can be a challenge—even for the best teachers and parents. If we can turn these tasks into meaningful games or play, we will have a much better chance at being successful. Two simple examples of cleaning up together are presented here to get you and your children started.

Bull's Eye

Description

This can be a fun way to put equipment away cooperatively at the end of a session of game playing. For this "game," ask the children to lift and carry a bench together (or whatever else they have been playing with) through an obstacle course (e.g., one or more hula hoops can be held by pairs of children to create a tunnel, and other obstacles can be used to create small mountains or manageable challenges). At the end of the obstacle course lies the storage area. All the equipment and all the children, including the ones holding the hoops, go through the hoops or other obstacles. To challenge the children to keep up a good pace, you can introduce a collective time for finishing the job.

Eco-Ball

Description

This game introduces an important concept of cooperation, not only with one another but also with the natural environment. After a cooperative games day, divide the play area into different sections. Each team takes a garbage bag (or two) and is responsible for cleaning up their section. The common goal is for everyone to work together to pick up all the litter, in or out of their area. A collective scoring system can be introduced if desired (e.g., one point for each piece of litter that originated with the games day and two points for litter that was there before).

3

Games for Children Ages 8 Through 12

As with the previous games, there is nothing sacred about the age category suggested for this chapter. Although we tested these games with children aged 8 to 12 and found them well received, some of the games presented (such as Log Roll and the cooperative bicycle tube games) are perfectly acceptable for 6-year-olds and 60-year-olds. Others (such as Collective Blanketball) are well received by older children, teenagers, and youthful adults, whatever their age. So stay flexible and open-minded when thinking about how to use these games and with whom.

The games presented here show how easy it is to make up new cooperative games or remake old games into new ones. Once you get started, you will find lots of opportunities to make joyful cooperation and full inclusion a part of the normal daily routine. From there on, kids will take their cue from you and from each other!

HIGHLIGHT GAMES

There are a number of highlight activities that focus on looking for the positives and finding good things in each other. The games work extremely well with the 8 to 12 age group and can be found in chapter 2 (see pages 13-15).

COOPERATIVE OUTDOOR ACTIVITIES

Outdoor activities can bring children and families together in fun-filled cooperative ventures. For those of you who have snow-filled winters, cooperative activities such as tobogganing, skating, or skiing together combined with winter picnics or winter camping are good options for building bonds and positive memories. In warmer months or climates, near lakes or oceans or rivers, canoeing or kayaking, tenting, and camping together are great options for joyful cooperative adventures. For those who live near mountains or trails, hiking, backpacking, trekking, and climbing provide lots of opportunities for people to link together in positive ways, where cooperation makes the journey much more joyful and the outcome much more positive.

COOPERATION IN THE PERFORMING ARTS

Other great opportunities for joyful cooperation (not specifically addressed in this book) include acting, dancing, singing, or making music together. Although there may be an element of competition in some of these domains, they all provide excellent opportunities for cooperation, collaboration, enjoyment, and personal development.

COOPERATIVE BICYCLE TUBE ACTIVITIES

Children can use old bicycle tubes to play lots of fun cooperative games. You can find tubes at any bicycle shop that does repairs. Ask the staff to save some of the old tubes, from changing tires that went flat, instead of throwing them out. Cut each tube on either side of the metal air valve, then tie the tube together in a knot. Now you have a round rubber tube without air in it, which is exactly what you need for these games. You need one tube for each pair of children. Sometimes we tie two tubes together into one round rubber tube, especially if the tubes are small. A great option for tube games is Thera-Band, a latex exercise band that is used for physiotherapy. You can buy it in rolls on the Internet or from medical supply stores. Here are a few co-op tube games to get you started.

Cooperative Sit-Ups

Equipment

One bicycle tube tied together for each pair of children

Description

Two children sit on the floor facing each other with the tube on top of their legs. Each player grabs hold of his side of the tube. They both lean back and lie down at the same time, then they both come back up to a sitting position at the same time. This resembles doing sit-ups together with the help of the tube. The children can do the exercise first with bent legs and then with straight legs. This game can also be played with two sets of partners using one tube.

Row Your Boat

Equipment

One bicycle tube tied together for each pair of children

Description

This game is similar to Cooperative Sit-Ups, where players sit on the floor and hold onto their side of the tube, but in this game as one player lies down, the other player sits up. They flow back and forth in this manner (and sometimes sing "Row, Row, Row Your Boat"). This game can also be played with two sets of partners using one tube.

Partner Tube Rebounding

Equipment

One bicycle tube tied together for each pair of children

Description

Partners begin this game by standing inside their tube, with the tube behind their backs. Both partners lean back to stretch the tube, then at the same time, use the stretched tube to propel themselves forward and exchange positions in the tube. Before exchanging positions, they need to decide whether they are both going to make the exchange on the right or left side of the other person. This form of cooperation will prevent midtube collisions. This game is lots of fun, and players will become creative with making exchanges and using the tube in unique ways.

Double Partner Tube Rebounding

Equipment

One bicycle tube tied together for every two pairs of children

Description

This game unfolds much like Partner Tube Rebounding except in this case four people begin inside one tube. Players 1 and 2 are on opposite sides of the tube, facing each other with the tube behind their backs. Players 3 and 4 are also inside the tube facing each other. Players 1 and 2 stretch the tube by leaning back and then rebound forward to exchange positions. Then players 3 and 4 stretch their sides of the tube and exchange positions. If they all work together, they can create a rhythmic sequence of each set of partners taking turns stretching the tube and rebounding to the other side. It is fun, creative, and cooperative.

ACTION GAMES

These are action games that most children love to play. The combination of action and cooperation keeps the games fun and the children moving.

Stomp and Shake

Equipment

One skipping rope or similar length of rope for every two children

Description

1. The children divide themselves into two groups: shakers and stompers.
2. The shakers each hold one end of an 8-foot (2.5-meter) rope (skipping ropes will do) between the thumb and first finger and squiggle the rope so that the other end drags along the floor.
3. When the game starts, shakers run around the play area, shaking the rope on the ground or floor behind them.
4. The Stompers run after the shakers and try to step on the end of one of the ropes, which usually pulls it loose from between the shaker's fingers. Once a stomper has stepped on a rope and it has fallen to the floor, the stomper picks it up and becomes a shaker. The shaker who just dropped the rope becomes a stomper, so their roles are reversed.

Helpful Tip

To keep the game moving, you may need to start with a few more stompers than shakers. It's a game of nonstop action—stomp and shake—and the kids enjoy it.

Hug Tag

Equipment

Ten brightly colored dish towels, ribbons, cloth pinnies, or beach balls

Description

This game has lots of action. The basic concept underlying this tag game is that a player is safe from being tagged only when she or he is hugging another player. There are lots of variations for how this game can be played, but the one I usually start with unfolds as follows.

1. For a group of about 20 children, start with 5 hug-its and 15 huggers. The hug-its are "It." Give each of them a ribbon, bright cloth, pinny, or beach ball.
2. The rest of the players are huggers. They start the game by spreading out around the room in pairs—each in contact with a partner.
3. When you or a designated leader yells, "Change!" the partners have to let go of each other and run to find someone else to hug. The hug-its try to tag the huggers while they are in the process of changing partners. If a child is tagged, she must take the ribbon or beach ball—she is now a hug-it. The person who tagged him runs to connect up with someone to be "safe." As long as a player is linked with one or more partners, he is safe. The moment a player is not in contact with someone, he can be tagged.
4. The leader continues to yell, "Change!" to keep the game moving.

Helpful Tip

Adjust the number of hug-its (up or down) during the game to make sure it is appropriately challenging for everyone—not too hard and not too easy. (Shoot for *approximately* one hug-it for every four players.) Young children and adults also enjoy this game, and it makes a great workout.

Frozen Tag

Description

If you want to play a tag game, why not introduce some helping components?

1. A few children are designated "freezers." While the rest of the children scatter in all directions, the freezers count to 10, then take off after the runners.

2. When a child is tagged, he freezes in a stride position with a hand extended out front. To unfreeze him, another child must either pass under his legs or shake his hand.
3. The number of freezers can be adjusted to keep the game moving.
4. When the children are tired or ready to play something else, the leader can end the game by asking the children, "How many of you unfroze your friends?" "How many people did you unfreeze?"

Variations

- Frozen Tag can also be played in pairs—with twin freezers, twin runners, twin freezes, and twin unfreezers. Partners hold hands and run together, freeze together, and unfreeze together, with both partners shaking hands with the frozen pair or going under the frozen pair's legs.
- The game can also be played in groups of three or in shallow water, where children run after each other splashing through the water and swim under each other's legs to unfreeze each other.

Crossover Dodgeball

Equipment

One soft, squishy ball or small pillow that does not hurt on impact for each two players (allow for a few extra balls, as necessary, in case any deflate)

Description

As in regular dodgeball, players begin on different sides of a line and attempt to throw soft, squishy balls or pillows at players on the other side. However, in this no-elimination version, if a player is hit with a ball or pillow, she immediately runs to the other side (to the other team) and continues to play. Players are continuously throwing balls, dodging balls, and switching sides. The objective of the game is for children to have fun in a safe context while improving their skills at throwing, anticipating, dodging, and running. The crossover structure, together with the additional balls and a moderate-sized playing area, ensures that everyone is always involved.

Variations

- You might present an additional challenge of seeing if they can end up with all players on one side, which requires a lot of hustling, or you might set the goal of having entire teams switch sides.
- The game can also be played in pairs (e.g., two throwing one pillow together at the same time or two with one towel tossing the ball or tossing another pillow).

Helpful Tips

- The game seems to work better with small teams.
- Adjust the number of players, the number of balls or pillows, the size of the playing area, and the rules as needed. If there are 5 players on a side (which is ideal), we generally use four beach balls, very soft rubber balls, or soft pillows. With 10 players per side, we have eight or nine balls (or pillows) in play.

TRUST GAMES

These are games that require an element of trust, along with lots of cooperation, to be played successfully. They are simple games, and children enjoy them.

Circle of Friends

Description

In this game, the children literally fall into the hands of their friends, who prevent them from hitting the floor.

1. About eight children kneel down (or stand) and form a tight circle, shoulder to shoulder.
2. The person standing in the middle of the circle stiffens her body and falls in any direction. Generally the middle person keeps her arms "glued" to her sides and is encouraged to not move her feet.
3. The children in the circle catch the person as she falls, then return her to an upright position.

4. Children take turns in the middle.

Helpful Tip

This game requires a collective effort and helps develop trust. The people forming the circle learn to work together to catch the middle person with their hands, to respectfully place their hands in appropriate spots, and to gently guide her in another direction. The person in the middle learns to trust that her friends will catch her gently and safely and keep her from falling. As proficiency increases, it is possible to back the circle up a bit (more room to fall).

Push 'Em Into Balance

Description

In traditional push-'em-out-of-balance games, two players face each other, grasp one or both hands, and try to push the other person off balance. If a person moves either foot, he loses. Push 'Em Into Balance reverses this process.

1. Two partners face each other, place the palms of their hands together, and take one step (or several steps) backward so that they are leaning on each other to maintain balance.
2. In unison, they attempt to push each other back up into balance (i.e., back up into standing) without moving their feet.

Variations

- As an additional challenge, try Partner Twirl. Players start the normal way hand to hand, but when they push against each other to return to their upright positions, they push hard and try to make one full rotation (twirl around) before reconnecting their hands.

- For a tougher challenge, try Partner Back-Up Twirl. Players begin seated back to back, with their knees bent and feet flat on the floor. By pushing against each other's backs, they come about halfway up to standing, and then, still leaning on each other to maintain balance, they turn or roll around to a leaning front-to-front position, ready for a series of standing push-up rebounds.

Helpful Tip

The basic Push 'Em Into Balance maneuver resembles a standing or leaning push-up done on a mirror, if you can visualize that. Players need to be careful to keep their feet secure on the floor or ground so they don't slip. Some children like to begin this game on their knees (rebounding while kneeling), gradually moving farther and farther apart and rebounding back up to an upright position on their knees. They can also try to come to a standing position from their knees by leaning into each other and pushing up from there.

PICNIC GAMES

Here are a few outdoor picnic games that can add some fun and challenge to the outing.

Watermelon Split

Equipment

A few watermelons

Description

If you want an active way to split up a watermelon or to work up a thirst before eating one—while encouraging some sharing initiatives—this may be the way. A whole watermelon is transported from one point to another in a relay fashion. It can be carried in a variety of ways (alone or with partners) before being handed off or tossed to fellow carriers. The important thing is for the players to work out their own plan to accomplish the goal together. Once the watermelon has been through the course, it is cut up and shared by all watermeloners. I'm sure they can think of some cooperative ventures for the watermelon seeds, such as a progressive or collective seed spit. For this one, it is best if each player spits her own seed from the point where the last one landed.

Cherry Bowl

Equipment

A few bowls of fresh cherries and some cherry pits

Description

A fruitful game for a picnic, party, or play day. Each player begins with about 10 cherry pits. Place a cherry pit in a shallow bowl or a shallow hole in the ground; each player then takes a turn trying to knock it out with his cherry pit. (The player can do this by placing the cherry pit on top of the index finger's fingernail, holding it there with the thumb. The player then snaps his finger off the thumb to send the cherry pit flying. The player could also simply throw the cherry pit, or, if available, throw marbles at the cherry pit.) Every time the pit is knocked out, every player gets to eat a cherry from a common supply. You can also fill the bowl with 20 cherry pits and have each player try to knock out as many as possible. If 2 (or 3) are knocked out, then each player gets 2 (or 3) cherries to eat, and so on, until the bowl is empty.

Fruit Cocktail

Equipment

A couple of bowls of tasty fruit; tools for cutting the fruit

Description

This is a good game for getting people together at a picnic or party. Bananas, apples, oranges, grapefruits, melons, or any other kinds of fruit are shared in this tasty game. Whole pieces of fruit are placed at one end of an open area, and the players carry or gently roll the fruit to a mixing area at the other end. Any number of people can work together to get the fruit to the mixing area, but they cannot use their hands, feet, or mouths. For example, an apple or banana or pineapple may be balanced on one bent-over back or between three people's fronts. Only when the fruit reaches the mixing area can it be eaten (and sometimes washed first depending on the type of journey it has endured). The players then divide the fruit up or make a fruit cocktail so that everyone enjoys eating it together. If you're near a lake, you might consider Floating Fruit Cocktail, where the fruit is nudged along in the water.

COLLECTIVE-GOAL GAMES

This section provides a variety of different kinds of collective-goal games where all players work and play together toward a common goal.

Esti-Time

Description

In this game, players estimate the time it will take them or their team to finish a specific task. Each participant or team makes their best guess on how long it will take, and the individual or team who finishes closest to the predicted time is the winner. This approach can be used in a variety of activities—going through an obstacle course, running, walking, swimming, paddling, cycling, skiing, orienteering, adventure racing, making a fire, cooking dinner, washing the dishes, getting dressed, cleaning up a bedroom, finishing a project, and so on.

This strategy takes the focus off the traditional way of "winning" (being the fastest) and directs it to the one who best knows her performing self. Let's take going for a run or getting dressed in the morning as an example. The players estimate the time it will take them to complete the distance or the task and see how close they come to their prediction. Looking at clocks or watches while performing is not allowed in this event.

This game of predicting times is also an interesting way of seeing how time goals influence people's performances. Sometimes just setting a time goal inspires people to move a little faster than normal. Before the players make a prediction for their next Esti-Time event, encourage them to draw lessons from the last one. Each player tries to improve on the accuracy of his last estimate—another way of winning.

Long, Long, Long Jump

Description

As the name implies, the objective of this activity is for a group of children to jump collectively as far as possible. The first player begins at a starting line and makes one jump. The next player starts his jump where the previous person landed. The players can attempt to better their total collective distance on successive tries. This game can be played indoors or out, with a forward long jump (standing or running); backward long jump; or hop, skip, and jump.

Log Roll

Description

1. A series of children (logs) lie side by side on their bellies on a mat, a rug, the grass, or any other comfortable surface.
2. A group of riders line up to get ready for the ride. A rider lies on her belly perpendicular to the logs, across the upper portion of their backs.
3. All the logs then begin rolling in the same direction, giving their rider a sometimes soft, sometimes bumpy ride across the top.

4. Once the rider has flopped over the last log, she becomes a rolling log at the end of the line of logs. This continues until they roll out of space or until they feel like stopping.
5. Players take turns being riders and logs.

Variations

- Two lightweight riders can try going across the rolling logs side by side. You might also want to try two lines of logs with two riders to keep things rolling along.
- Two rows of stretched-out logs hold hands between lines as they roll. Once it gets rolling, it's a fun game for young and old alike.

Helpful Tips

- If a larger log would prefer not to take the ride, he can just pass on the ride and continue being a log.
- A heavier rider on light logs can go slowly and support some of his own weight along the way, by putting his hands on the ground between the logs.

Towering Tower

Equipment

An assortment of materials children can use to build a tower, such as cardboard boxes, plastic containers, and anything else that might be handy

Description

The objective of this game is for children to work together to build a single tower out of beanbags, cardboard boxes, hoops, balls, old shoes, or any other materials you have handy. To add a physically active component to the game, the children can run (skip, hop, crabwalk) around the play area until the leader calls, "Tower!" At this point, each child gets one piece of equipment of her choice from a common supply and places it in the middle of the play area to help build the tower. The children then run around until "Tower!" is called again before adding further material to the towering tower.

I remember one of the first times we played this game with a group of 8-year-olds at school. Just before the dismissal bell rang, they managed to place the last block on their towering tower, which had a distinct lean to it. All the children in the class jumped up and down, cheering. They all contributed, and they all felt good about their collective creation.

Variations

- Children can also pair up for this game, and when "Tower!" is called, they select and carry a piece of equipment to the tower site together. If you're using large building blocks, this is functional and may be necessary. If you're not, try having the children carry the building blocks balanced on two sticks or held between their bodies. At certain intervals, when "Tower!" is called, players can select a new partner to work with.
- For additional challenge, consider using very large cardboard boxes, which you can get from appliance or grocery stores. The question will be "How are we going to get this way up there?" They'll find a way.

Box Ball

Equipment

One soccer-type ball or ball that can be kicked on the ground and one skipping rope or similar length of rope for every four children

Description

Box Ball is played by four children working as a unit to keep a rope taut in the shape of a box while moving a ball from one base to another. First they just practice moving the ball along the floor or ground with their feet while walking and holding the rope taut in the shape of a square.

1. To play the real game of Box Ball, teams of four with ropes are scattered around the playing area at different bases.
2. Each team of four kicks its ball to the next base, leaves the ball there, and runs back to its original base to get the ball that was dropped off by another team. The children must move the ball while keeping it within the confines of their taut rope.
3. This ball-moving process continues until each team has its original ball back.

Variation

For additional challenge, the time it takes for all balls to complete the circuit can be recorded, and all players can then get together to discuss how to help each other improve their collective time before playing the next game.

Over and Over

Equipment

A couple of medicine balls, exercise balls, or beach balls

Description

1. Players form two lines, about four kid-lengths apart. The first person in each line has a beach ball (or medicine ball or rubber exercise ball), which he passes backward over his head to the next person in line.
2. The first person in each line who just passed the ball over his head immediately turns around and slaps one hand with the second person ("gimme five"), who must momentarily free one hand from the ball, balancing it with the other.
3. The first person in each line then runs to the end of the other line, where another ball is being passed along.
4. The second person in the line (who is now first) repeats this procedure, and so it goes over and over down the line. The common objective is to move both balls and both lines from one point to another as quickly as possible, perhaps from one end of the gym to the other.

Variations

- Is variety possible in Over and Over? Of course it is! The children can form two double lines, and partners use their inside arms only to pass the ball over their heads to the next set of partners, or partners lie on their backs side by side and use their inside legs only to pass a beach ball over their heads to the set of partners behind. The high five is optional in this one. If the ball drops, players just pick it up (with their hands) and continue from where they left off.

- Another variation of Over and Over is called Under and Under. It is basically the same game except the children pass the ball under their legs instead of over their heads.

Carry On

Equipment

One beach ball and one base for every four players (the base can be anything you can put on the ground or floor to serve as home base)

Description

1. Four players and one beach ball start at each base. (The total number of bases depends on the number of players.)
2. Two players from each base attempt to move their beach ball to the next base with their bodies, without using their hands and without kicking the ball (e.g., hip to hip or belly to back).
3. They then pass the ball to the set of partners remaining at the next base (without using their hands), await the delivery of another ball from their partners behind them, and continue around the bases. The second two children start out as soon as the two children from another base deliver a ball to them.

Variation

For something a little more strenuous, teams of three or five are formed at various equally spaced bases. The objective is to get all players from one base to the next by carrying them. If three players start on each base, two of them carry the first person (player 1) to the next base and then run back to their starting point (their home base). The newly delivered person at their home base helps carry their second team member (player 2) to the next base. On the next delivery, their third team member (player 3) will be dropped off (or occasionally dragged) by two team members who moved up from the base behind their home base. This process continues until members of all teams have been moved to another base. It's a fun game that can be played in snow or mud for additional messy fun and challenge.

Ladder Travel

Equipment

One sturdy ladder, bench, or plank for each group of about 10 players

Description

This game uses another form of movement with human support.

1. Players spread out along both sides of a sturdy ladder, bench, or plank and lift it up so it is held horizontally below their waists, with straight arms. The players at one end of the ladder bend their legs and lower that end of the ladder to the ground so that the "traveler" can step or crawl on it.
2. The ladder is then slowly brought back up to a horizontal position, and the traveler walks or crawls across. Once he reaches the other end, the children on this end lower the ladder so he can get off.
3. The traveler then becomes a carrier for the next traveler.

Variation

Depending on the size and strength of the players, some groups may be able to hold the ladder horizontally at shoulder height, with safety precautions (such as making sure strong people carry the ladder, and that one or two people act as spotters and follow the ladder in case the carriers need additional support). Ladder carriers can also walk around with the traveler sitting or crawling on the ladder or gently rock the ladder back and forth.

QUIET GAMES

The quiet cooperation games create a different and calmer atmosphere within the group and provide a nice break from the more active games.

Silent Birthday Lineup

Description

Ask everyone in the room (children and adults) to line up according to the month and day of their birth, "without any talking." Using fingers, toes, or hand gestures is fine, but written and verbal communication is not allowed. Ready . . . go! This will inspire some interesting means of communication toward a common goal.

Aura

Description

Can human auras really draw people together? Here's a chance to find out. Partners stand facing each other and stretch their arms out in front until their palms are gently touching. Ask the players to see if they can feel the energy or warmth of the other person's aura by focusing on the feeling in their hands. Both partners then close their eyes, lower their hands, and try to reconnect the palms of their hands, keeping their eyes closed.

Variation

- When players are successful at the basic activity, they can lower their hands, keep their eyes closed, and turn in place two or three times before trying to reconnect by touching the palms of their hands.
- Play this game with three or more by asking the children to form a circle together.

Tweetie

Description

1. All eyes are closed. Whisper in one person's ear, "You're the tweetie." The tweetie remains silent throughout the game.
2. Keeping eyes closed, each person finds another's hand, shakes it, and asks, "Tweetie?"
3. If both players ask, "Tweetie?" the two drop hands and go on to someone else. A player who gets no response to the question has found the tweetie and becomes part of the tweetie by holding on to the tweetie's hand and remaining silent from then on. Anyone shaking hands with any member of the tweetie becomes a part of it, and the tweetie grows larger and larger until everyone in the room is holding hands. Once the group has become one giant tweetie, ask all the children to open their eyes.

Helpful Tip

To avoid problems in finding the tweetie, keep the size of the play space small, and ask the tweetie bird to give out a chirp now and then.

Draw and Sing a Song

Equipment

One large sheet of paper and a box of crayons or markers for each group of five players; slips of paper with the names of songs written on them

Description

We usually play this in groups of about five or six children.

1. Give each group one large sheet of paper along with some crayons or markers.
2. One player from each group then chooses one of several slips of paper on which you have written the titles of songs well known to the children. Each slip of paper contains the name of a different song.
3. The player then brings this paper back to her group, and with or without speaking, the children draw clues to that particular song.
4. The other groups of children try to guess the song title from the creative clues drawn on the sheet of paper. When someone guesses the song, all groups stand up, join arms, and sing the song.

Variations

- This game can be adapted to draw clues to historical events, countries, famous people, and so on.
- It can also be played in pairs or trios, according to the size of the group.

Candle Carry

Equipment

One candle for every four or five players and something to light the candle (a lighter or wooden matches)

Description

Here is a relay for older children or adults that favors those with a moderate pace. A lighted candle is carried through a course and passed from player to player while tricycling, bicycling, walking, swimming, or jogging. Too swift a pace may extinguish the flame, and too slow a pace may result in the flame extinguishing itself (running out of candle). A fun game to play in a safe area with appropriate supervision, especially when it is beginning to get dark. We have played this game safely and successfully on a sandy beach and in other settings where there is no risk of burning anything.

HUMAN TANGLES

The following two games attempt to bring people together by having them work as a unit to untangle themselves. These untangling games may also be played in shallow water, where they more closely resemble human spaghetti.

Human Knot

About 10 players stand in a circle, place their hands in the center, and take hold of the hands of two people other than those immediately next to them. Then the group works together in an attempt to untie the knot without releasing handholds. It is a little more manageable if players do not grasp hands with people directly across from them.

Human Pretzel

All but two players hold hands in a circle and twist themselves over and under and through one another without dropping hands. The two other people, who have had their backs turned to the pretzel-making process, then try to untangle the group. The pretzel cooperates as the untanglers try to figure out who and what goes where and how.

WATER GAMES

With proper supervision and diligent water-safety precautions, water is an excellent medium for cooperative games, both in the natural outdoors and in a pool. Many of the games presented in this book can be adapted for play in water, as well as in mud, sand, fields, playgrounds, or snow.

Any time you are around water or are playing games in water, it is essential that you have competent adults to closely watch and supervise the children at all times. Specific competent people should be assigned to cover specific areas at specific times so that there is always someone watching to ensure the safety of everyone.

Water Cup Pass

Equipment

One paper or plastic cup for each player

Description

Players stand in a circle with an empty paper cup in their teeth. One player's cup is filled with water. This person begins by pouring her water into the cup of the next person without using her hands. He then pours it into the next person's cup without using his hands. This water-passing process continues all the way around the circle. See how much water remains at the end.

Variation

For more involvement, more players can start with filled cups, or smaller circles can be formed.

Water Bridge

Description

The objective of this game is to use all players to get one person across the shallow end of the pool without carrying him and without him going into the water. There is more than one way to do this. Here's an example: Players form two lines across the shallow end of the pool. The players in each line face one another and grasp wrists with the person across from them, forming a bridge. One person begins to crawl across the bridge (on hands and knees) but may run out of bridge unless the people forming the first part of the bridge run to the end as soon as the crawler has passed them.

Variations

- For younger groups, a story can be made up as to why the player (animal, princess, or whatever) going across the ladder must not get wet (e.g., "cats don't like water" or "the princess has her party dress on").
- For older groups, the two lines of people can also try to pass a person at shoulder level from one inner-tube island to another.

Log Chute

Description

1. The children form two lines in the shallow end of the pool, with the people in each line facing each other and joining hands with the person across from him.
2. All players move their arms in a circular motion, just below the surface of the water, toward the end of the lines.
3. As the water begins to churn down the chute (the area between the two lines), one by one the people at the front of the lines float above the arms and down the current in the chute while lying on their backs.
4. They then move to the end of the chute, join hands, and keep the current moving for the next pair to chute.

Whirlpool

Description

Players form one large circle near one corner of the pool. The people in the circle join hands and move the whole circle around by walking as briskly as possible. As the water begins to ripple and the current begins to build up, people take turns breaking off and floating along with the moving water away from the circle. The group can also form one large circle near the middle of the shallow end of the pool and, once the circle is moving fast, all let go at the same time, floating outward on their backs with the current.

Water-Balloon Toss

Equipment

One or two small balloons that can be filled with water for each player

Description

Partners stand about 3 feet (1 meter) apart and toss a small balloon filled with water back and forth. After each round (two tosses), partners take a step backward. If the balloon bursts and a child gets soaked, naturally she will want to share this with her partner. Just tell her to give her partner a big hug. It's a fun game to play outside on a hot summer day.

COLLECTIVE-SCORE GAMES

The idea of two or more individuals or groups working together toward mutually beneficial ends is central to cooperative play and games. Collective scoring is one means of encouraging two or more teams to play cooperatively toward a common end. In this context, neither team achieves success by competing against the other or at the expense of another; rather, both win as a result of playing together.

As with other cooperative games, flexibility is an important component of collective-score games. People with various skills and abilities can play, and the number of players per side is adaptable. Because teams are not fixed and rigid or pitted against each other, the children are free to change sides. Players can choose to serve the ball or play it from anywhere they wish. They can propel the ball with anything they want and in any manner. Any number of balls can be used, of any size or shape, including beach balls, exercise balls, pushballs (or monsterballs), regular balloons, or weather balloons. Standards (uprights to which nets are attached) can be 20 feet (6 meters) high or a few inches (10 centimeters) high. Nets can be sloped, slooped, or even crisscrossed to form a large *X*, with one team in each of the four quadrants. The variations for collective play are limitless when you let your imagination run free. Let your children's imaginations run free as well as they lead you in new ways for playing together cooperatively, for fun, with acceptance, and with inclusion.

Togeth-Air Ball (Collective-Score Volleyball)

Equipment

A beach ball, balloon, or volleyball and a net or rope for every two teams of players

Description

An early version of this game was played by the Caribou Eskimo in the 1800s. The objective was to keep a sealskin ball in motion without letting it touch the ground. No score was kept. In the contemporary version, two teams stand on either side of a line, rope, or net and bat a ball back and forth in a continuous fashion. If a score is kept, let it be collective. Children initially count one point whenever anyone hits the ball, seeing how many times they can hit the ball before it touches the ground. Team members from both sides can also chant out loud the number of consecutive hits and encourage each other along the way. At most age levels, players can be encouraged to "coach" each other to improve their collective ball-handling skills.

Variations

- Three different team members or even all team members could hit the ball ("all touch") before it goes over the net. "All touch" works best with sides of three, four, or five each.
- Try playing with unlimited hits per side, with points scored only when the ball goes over the net.
- Put two balls into play at the same time.
- Instead of counting hits, players can see how long (seconds or minutes) they can keep the ball going back and forth.
- Players can use the backs of their hands, their fists, their elbows, their heads, rackets, branches, air pumps, water shooters, plastic bats, Frisbees, fans, and the like to keep the ball up.
- Another approach is to lower the net (or rope) so that a small beach ball, rubber ball, or tennis ball can be bounced back and forth. The objective here is to hit the ball back and forth as many times as possible, either on the bounce or on the fly. Participants can use their open hands or paddleball rackets to propel the ball. Come up with your own variations.

Helpful Tip

For people who are not skilled at ball handling, it is a good idea to start this game with a balloon or beach ball before going on to something more difficult, such as a volleyball.

Bump and Scoot

Equipment

A beach ball and a net or rope for every two teams of players

Description

We rarely divide groups based on gender alone. However, in one school we found that the boys in the fourth and fifth grades complained about playing with the girls, and the girls complained about playing with the boys because when they did play together, the boys would always hog the ball. In an attempt to solve this problem, we came up with the following game.

Boys start on one side of a net and girls on the other. Whenever a person on one team hits the beach ball over the net, she or he scoots under the net to the other side. Rather than a collective score, the common objective is to make a complete change in teams with as few drops of the ball as possible. A complete change of teams in this case means that all the boys end up on the side of the net where the girls started, and all the girls end up on the side of the net where the boys started. This was the collective goal, and it could be accomplished only through cooperation.

When we played Bump and Scoot with these children, a very interesting thing occurred. Boys started to "feed" girls the ball, girls started to feed boys the ball, teams became happily integrated, and everyone played together in order to help all team members exchange sides.

Variation

This game can also be played for a collective score only, where all players attempt to keep the ball (or balls) going back and forth as many times as possible as they scoot back and forth as many times as possible. Adapt it any way you want to make it work best for your group.

Helpful Tip

Bump and Scoot works best and moves more quickly when there are not too many players on each team. With a class or larger group, it is best to have several games going at once in different parts of the gym.

Bump and Team Scoot

Equipment

A beach ball and a net or rope for every four teams of players

Description

Bump and Team Scoot provides lots of action, particularly with larger groups. The overall objective is to score as many consecutive collective bump and scoots as possible.

1. Four teams are formed. Teams 1 and 2 start on one side of the net, and teams 3 and 4 start on the other side. Each team chooses a code name or team name.

2. When a player hits the ball over the net, she yells her team's code name, and her whole team scoots under the net with her.
3. When the next player hits the ball over the net, he yells his team's code name, and his whole team scoots under the net with him. This game keeps everyone scooting, especially if you use two balls.

Variation

Another option for Bump and Team Scoot is for only team members who touched the ball on the rally, or helped set the ball up, to scoot under the net when the ball is bumped over.

Blanketball

Equipment

A sturdy blanket and a beach ball or soft rubber ball for each team of players

Description

1. Teams of about eight players spread out around a sturdy blanket or similar-sized piece of durable material.
2. Players grasp the edges of the blanket, and a beach ball or other soft ball is placed in the middle.
3. To warm up, the group tosses the ball in the air and catches it again in the blanket. They can also try rolling the ball around the outside edges of the blanket so it touches their fingers without rolling off the blanket.
4. Two teams of eight, each around their own blanket, can then attempt to pass one ball back and forth by tossing it in unison toward the receiving team.

Variations

- If the players are successful at the basic activity of passing one ball between teams, you can give each team its own ball, and the players can try to exchange balls by simultaneously tossing toward the other team on a signal that is agreed on.
- Another blanket option is for one team to toss the ball straight up, high in the air, and dash out of the way to let the other team dash in under the ball to catch it with the blanket. This requires a collective awareness and a cooperative effort.
- Groups seeking additional challenge can try juggling (keeping two or more balls going in the air in a continuous manner). This can be attempted initially by one team alone, making sure one of

two balls is always in the air, and later by tossing balls from team to team.

- To involve more people, use more teams or a larger blanket (e.g., a sturdy bedspread, a large piece of lightweight canvas, or a small parachute).

Collective-Score Blanketball

Equipment

A sturdy blanket, a beach ball or soft rubber ball, and a net or rope for every two teams of players

Description

Two teams use a blanket to toss a beach ball (or other large lightweight ball) back and forth over a rope or volleyball net. Every time one team tosses the ball over the net and the other team successfully catches it, one collective point is scored.

This game is extremely cooperative in structure because every team member is a part of every toss and every catch made by the team. In addition, both teams work together toward a common end, and success is possible only through cooperation. The collective challenge of scoring as many points in a row as possible keeps most players engaged in the process of working together and in the hunt for a higher score.

A variety of age groups have received this game very well. We once had three different Collective-Score Blanketball games going all at once, taking up the whole length of a large gym. At one point I looked up from behind a monsterball and saw another monsterball being tossed sideways to an adjoining team on the same side of the gym. Another group had two beach balls going through the air at the same time. Players were having fun experimenting with different-sized balls, blankets, and even beach towels. It was a very special feeling for me to see these children and youth of such diverse backgrounds and skill levels playing together joyfully—with everyone included. It was also very satisfying to see that they were thinking and playing outside of the box.

All on One Side

Equipment

One balloon and a net or rope for each team of players

Description

Have you ever heard of a volleyball game that starts with a team of four or five players on one side of the net and no team on the other side? No? Well, now you have. The objective of this game is to get your team to the other side of the net and back as many times as possible.

1. Using a balloon for a ball, each player bumps or taps the balloon to another player and then scoots under the net to the other side. The last player to touch the balloon taps it over the net and scoots under the net.
2. The receiving players try to keep the balloon in play by tapping it to another player on their side of the court and scooting under the net—repeating the entire side-changing process.

Variation

As the team gets better, try putting two balloons (or beach balls or even volleyballs) into play at one time.

Collective-Score Monsterball

Equipment

One large rubber ball, exercise ball, or monsterball and a net or rope for every two teams of players

Description

This collective-score volleyball-type game uses a large rubber ball, an exercise ball, or a canvas-covered rubber ball, sometimes called a pushball or monsterball. In this game, players on each side of the net lift, push, tap, or propel the ball back and forth over the rope or net. Each time the ball goes over the net, a collective point is scored. The larger ball increases the number of people directly involved in getting it up and over the net because players often need the help of teammates.

Helpful Tips

- If teams are large, try putting more than one ball into play.
- You can also use a weather balloon (see your local weather reporter), or you can order a big rubber exercise ball through your local sporting goods or fitness equipment store or on the Internet.

Balloon Bucket (Collective Hoops)

Equipment

One balloon or beach ball and one hula hoop for each pair of children

Description

1. Spread the hula hoops on the floor around the playing area.
2. Partners tap a balloon back and forth to each other in a nonstop fashion as they attempt to get to a hoop, pick it up, tap their balloon through it, and replace it on the floor. Partners must keep moving in the direction of different hula hoops while continuing to tap their balloon back and forth.
3. The objective of the game is for the entire group to collectively score as many hoops as possible in a certain time period (e.g., 5 minutes).

4. Players can run, but they cannot run while holding a balloon, and they cannot tap the balloon twice in succession. It must be hit by one partner and then the other. They must continue to move from hoop to hoop and can return to the same hoop only after they have tapped their balloon through all the other hoops. Each set of partners keeps track of their own score (how many hoops they scored), and the collective group score is added up at the end.

Variations

- This totally active game requires total involvement and a great deal of cooperation. It can be played with groups of any size merely by adjusting the number of hoops that are put out. It can also be played in teams of three rather than in pairs.
- To add a little more challenge, see if the players can get themselves and their balloon through each hoop.

Collective Orbit

Equipment

One large lightweight ball, exercise ball, or monsterball for each team of players

Description

1. One group of players forms one large circle, and another group of players forms a smaller circle inside the other. The inside players lie down on their backs (on mats, grass, sand, or the floor), with their heads pointing toward the center of the circle and their feet propped up in a bicycling position. The outside players stand with hands and arms ready for action.
2. The objective of the game is for all the players to work together to keep a large lightweight ball, exercise ball, or monsterball in play while moving it around the circle. The ball alternates between the

inside players, who use their feet to balance and move the ball, and the outside players, who push it back in and keep it moving around the circle with their hands. An attempt is made by both teams to keep the ball moving and prevent it from touching the ground. The number of times the ball moves around the circle can be counted aloud.

Variation

For additional action, a beach ball can be passed around the outside circle (using hands) while the larger exercise ball or monsterball is in play.

Collective Rounders

Equipment

Five bases and a ball that can be kicked, batted, or thrown

Description

This total-inclusion game with no losers centers on batting, fielding, and scoring in a cooperative way.

1. Spread out four or five bases on the field or floor.
2. One person (a batter or kicker) starts at home plate and propels an object (usually a ball) into the playing field by batting, kicking, or throwing it. She then proceeds to run around the bases as quickly as possible. She must circle completely around each base (rather than just touch it) before proceeding on to the next base.
3. One of the fielders closest to the ball picks it up (or traps it with his foot), and the ball is then passed around to all other players in the field, either by throwing it or kicking it. When the last person in the field touches the ball, he yells, "Freeze!" The batter must then stop stone-cold and freeze in her tracks, no matter where she is, even if she is between two bases.
4. Another player then goes up to home plate; bats, kicks, or throws the ball; and starts to round the bases. Any "frozen" runners on the field can continue their circuit around the bases once the ball is batted, kicked, or thrown into the playing field by the next batter. Each batter tries to get as far around the bases as possible before someone yells, "Freeze!"
5. A point is scored every time a person completes the full circuit around all the bases. The game usually continues until the collective score equals the number of players, which should mean that every player has scored one point.

Variations

- This game can be played as a modified version of field hockey or ice hockey by shooting a soft ball or spongy puck with a hockey stick into the field, or kickball by kicking a ball into the field, or inner-tube water polo by throwing the ball from one tube into a field of floating players on tubes, or broomball by sweeping a ball into the field.
- The players can use a Frisbee, beach ball, beanbag, water balloon, exercise ball, small medicine ball, softball, football, or whatever they decide.

Helpful Tips

- The number of bases and the distance they are spread apart is adaptable depending on the game being played, the players' skill level, and the number of participants. Adjustments can be made once the game has started so that the time to complete the circuit with a well-placed ball and the time for fielders to pass the ball to everyone are very close.
- Fielders can experiment with different methods to pass the ball to one another. They can all run toward the ball and quickly pass it to one another; they can stay in their positions on the field, letting the closest person trap the ball and then pass it around; they can all run toward the ball, form a line, and pass the ball from person to person under their legs; and so on.

Jim's Rounders

Equipment

Five bases and a ball that can be kicked, batted, or thrown

Description

This is an example of how Jim Deacove (who has been creating innovative cooperative table games for many years—see the resource section) put a cooperative twist on the traditional game of children's baseball. As in competitive baseball, there are two teams. Here, however, each team stays up at bat until it scores the number of runs equal to the number of players on the team. If there are five players on a team, they must get five runs to fill the quota. If a grounder is hit, the batter advances one base; on an infield fly, two bases; on an outfield fly, three bases. When runners are on base, they are bumped up or moved ahead as their teammates get hits.

Now here's the clincher! For a hit to count, the team in the field must successfully stop a ground ball before it stops rolling or catch a fly ball before it hits the ground. Remember, the fielders are trying to get the ball to ensure that the batter gets on base, not to put the other team out.

For one team to fill its quota, it needs the help of the other team. For the fielding team to get up to bat, they need to help the batting team fill its quota. Batters generally get three pitches and rotate back into the order if they don't get a hit; but the pitcher has a reason to throw hittable balls. Fielders rotate through the different positions during the course of the game.

Variation

For players who are younger, less skilled, or new to the game of baseball, this game can be played as a modified version of tee ball, where the ball is placed on a chest-high, stationary upright tee (semiflexible plastic pipe works well as an upright). The batter swings until she bats the ball (tees off) into play.

REVERSE-SCORE GAMES

If you want to introduce a novel twist that really plays with the contemporary concept of winning and losing, try a reverse-score game. Every time one team scores, the other team gets a point. It's a gift! This will lead to some confused looks but may also get some players focused on just playing the game and enjoying the process of playing and scoring, without worrying about anything else. If you want to move further outside the traditional box, have the players who score switch to the winning team, which is the team with the most points, but it's actually the weaker team because it got its points by being scored on. When it's all over, try asking who won!

GAMES FOR RELAXATION AND STRESS CONTROL

Games that teach children of all ages how to relax and control stress can be of great value because children can use these skills in a variety of situations for the rest of their lives. Relaxation games focus on teaching children how to cooperate with their own minds and bodies. Participants learn how to talk to themselves in positive ways and connect with their bodies, their muscles, and their breathing to calm down and relax. Following are two of my favorite games for this age group to encourage relaxation.

Special Place Relaxation

Equipment

Audio CD player and audio CD *Changing Channels: Positive Living Skills for Children* (see Resources, page 160)

Description

In this activity, children imagine they are in a very special place that is calm and safe and totally relaxing. Children begin by lying down on the floor or by relaxing in their chairs. Ask them to do the following: "Breathe in slowly. Breathe out slowly. Let yourself relax. In your mind you are going to go to a very special place, a place that is warm and beautiful and totally relaxing. It can be a real place that you love to visit or a special place that you make up in your mind. In your special place you feel calm, and relaxed, and in control. In your special place you feel great. You can go there any time you want to find peace and tranquility." On this audio CD series, these relaxation sequences are presented in more detail and accompanied by relaxing music. The activities teach children specific skills for relaxation and stress control and leave the children feeling good, calm, and completely relaxed.

Changing Channels

Equipment

Audio CD player and audio CD *Changing Channels: Positive Living Skills for Children* (see Resources, page 160)

Description

In this activity, children lie down or relax in their chairs and listen to a story. Begin by asking them to do the following: "Get yourself into a comfortable position. Breathe in slowly. Breathe out slowly. Let yourself relax." Then ask them to listen to the story "Changing Channels." Here is the basis of the story: "You have many different channels in your mind—stressed channels, relaxed channels, happy channels, worry channels, positive channels, negative channels, focused channels, and not focused channels. You have the power to control what channel you are on. You can choose to be on a positive channel or a relaxed channel or a focused channel by deciding to do it. And you can change channels in your mind if you get on to a channel that is not helping you or those around you. Decide what channel you want to be on today. Click on to that channel now, and stay there for the rest of the day."

These audio CD activities are an effective way of teaching children how to relax, how to control their stress, and how to focus and be on a positive channel more often. If you are interested in getting complete scripts and a series of audio CD activities for teaching children to relax and control their stress, see my book *Feeling Great: Teaching Children to Excel at Living,* and consult the positive living skills audio CDs in the Resources at the end of this book.

4

Games for Preschoolers

When I first started to spend most of my days playing with groups of preschool children (30 years ago), I remember wondering how I was going to get a group of excited little kids quietly together in one spot, let alone get them to cooperate in a game. But I persisted, and together we taught each other, we adapted our ways, we stretched our brains, and we scaled down our games. I learned a great deal from those children, and as a result, some very interesting and gratifying things emerged over the following years. I was inspired by the fact that the children learned to cooperate not only within the games but also outside the games, as acts of togetherness began to fill their unstructured play.

After many years of creating and teaching little people's cooperative games, I turned my attention to creating activities to teach young children how to relax, focus, reduce stress, listen attentively, respect themselves, and be nice to each other. I believe that if we teach young children skills for cooperation and empathy as well as skills for relaxation, stress control, and seeing the positives in themselves and others, we give them a true gift that they can carry with them for life.

Whenever I play cooperative games with children now, I always end the session with an activity that teaches skills for relaxation, stress control, or positive thinking. I ask the children to sit or lie down quietly, and together we listen to a relaxation exercise or activity in positive living skills designed specifically for young children. We then discuss how they can apply the skill they just learned—in their own day and own lives. This concludes the cooperative games session on a very positive and uplifting light. If you are interested in getting complete scripts and a series of audio CD activities for teaching children to relax and control their stress, see my book *Feeling Great: Teaching Children to Excel at Living,* and consult the CDs on positive living skills in the resource section at the end of this book.

I learned some important lessons from teaching cooperative activities to 3- and 4-year-old children that are applicable to older children as well.

- **Develop a normal pregame routine that the children follow whenever they enter the play environment.** Children benefit from a certain amount of structure in readying themselves for listening to instructions and playing cooperative games within this context. For example, place two colored mats (boats) or thin rugs (magic carpets) in the middle of the play space. Explain to the children that as soon as they enter the play space, they should walk, skip, or crawl right over to those boats or magic carpets, sit down, and wait there for instructions. Or as soon as they walk into the gym, they can run around the gym twice, being careful to not bump into anyone, and then go directly to the red circle in the middle of the play area and sit down to wait for instructions. It helps to give children a specific routine and place to go as soon as they enter that play zone, especially when they are excited about playing—which they usually are. Although it is important that the children have lots of time to run around and play, it is also important that they listen to instructions so they know how to play the games you are introducing.

- **Gain the children's full attention before introducing a game. Ask them to focus fully on you—with their eyes, ears, and bodies.** Gaining young children's focus long enough to introduce a game is sometimes a challenge. Once the children are sitting down on the mats or in the circle, I join the circle as well and ask them to focus on me. I ask them to look at my eyes ("I want to see your eyes"), to listen with their ears and their eyes and their bodies. I want their eyes facing me, the front of their bodies facing me (with their hands and legs still), and their ears wide open to hear about the game we are going to play. I call this a full-body focus, and it enhances learning at all age levels. When there is no focus, there is no learning. I begin every playing session by asking for their focus. When some children are focusing really well, I point this out to the group and comment on how well they are focusing with their eyes, ears, and bodies.

- **Break down instructions for playing the games into very simple, understandable steps.** If things are not presented clearly and simply, the children will not know what to do, and the game generally will not work. This usually becomes obvious within the first 30 seconds or minute of play. Often you can correct things right there at that moment by stopping and reexplaining the game. Make sure you break the game down into tiny little steps.

- **Show the children what you are asking them to do by guiding a few children through the actions while the others watch.** For example, if you are introducing cooperative balloons through hoops, take a group of four children. Place one child on each side of the hoop with one hand holding the hoop. Place the other two children across from each other so they are looking at each other through the hole in the hoop. Give them a balloon and let them tap it through the hole in the hoop. At this age, a clear visual image is worth more than a thousand words.

- **Remain ready to either scale down the challenge of the game or increase the challenge, depending on how the group is responding.** Adapt the game to meet the children's needs and level of maturity instead of trying to adapt the children to fit the game.

- **Find a way to regain the children's attention after they have finished playing their first game, so you can comment on the good things they did in that last game and introduce the next game.** When children are excited, it is not always easy to get them to refocus on what you want to say. One approach that we have found successful with young children is to use a tambourine. At the beginning of the play session, I explain that I will need their attention to tell them about the new games we will be playing during our time together. I show them the tambourine and bang on the tambourine three times. This is their signal to freeze in place and drop down on one knee (one knee on the floor, one foot on the floor). We practice doing it a few times. I ask them to run around the play area, being sure not to bump into anyone else, and to "freeze" in the one-knee-down "full focusing position" when I bang the tambourine three times. It works well and saves your voice. I do not yell at the children; I wait until they are still, ask for their focus, and begin the instructions for the next activity when they face me with full focus.

- **Join in the activity by playing with the children, at least until they are familiar with the game.** I enjoy playing the games with the

Enjoying some connected cooperative time together in the outdoors.

children, and they enjoy having me play with them, so I almost always join in their play. It gives a firsthand look at how the game is working and moving and how it feels on the inside. It is not a requirement for a successful cooperative games session, but it is a bonus if you are comfortable taking that step.

- **Draw out the lessons from each cooperative games session. Think about what went well and what could be improved.** I think about specific games that went well and what made them work. I think about games that didn't go as well as I had anticipated and what could make them flow better. I think about my interaction with the group of children and with individual children—what worked well and where I could be better or more positive or more supportive.

My goal with cooperative games has always been for all children to happily engage in these activities because I believe they can all gain something of value through this involvement. One surprising challenge I faced early in my career with preschool children was that a couple of children chose not to join in the cooperative play. These children were often the ones who could have benefited most from the experience. They generally did not have well-developed skills for interacting with others in positive ways, and some also worried that they would not be accepted or included in the games. These kinds of fears are usually based on some previous experience that was hurtful.

On one occasion, Keith, a little lad of four, sat on the sidelines the moment he entered the gym. The classroom teacher informed me that Keith was not well coordinated and was probably "afraid to join in" the games. A mere four years in this world and already acutely aware that games are for the skilled! What do I do in such situations?

First I try to personally encourage the child to join in: "Come on, Keith, these are fun games; you'll like them." If that doesn't work, I send other kids over to try to recruit him, especially if a game requires two or three players. Next I ask the child to be my partner. That sometimes works, sometimes does not.

If I continue to meet with these "I don't wanna play" challenges (which has been rare in my experience), there is one thing I feel I have going for me: I make sure the kids always come into the gym or play area even if they do not want to play any games. I know that they watch the other kids play and that with time they will see that it's fun, that everyone is accepted, and that they don't have to worry about being the best (or most skilled) to be totally accepted and of value in the game. They also learn how the games are played and how the children play together as a unit to make the games work. I wait and watch and encourage and wait some more. These reluctant children wait and watch and wait some more. In the end, they almost always choose to get involved within one or two cooperative games sessions. In Keith's case, after 8 weeks he joined in his first game on his own accord. I breathed a sigh of relief. Fortunately he still holds the time record, and I am glad I never gave up on him. Once Keith got into the games, he became one of the most enthusiastic players, and he gained a lot of confidence from those experiences.

Sometimes we need to remind ourselves to patiently wait for progress. The children with whom we are working and playing come from all kinds of different backgrounds, personal experiences, and home situations. It takes more time and focus to bring some of those children along, but in the end they all gain from following a path with heart.

What is crystal clear from my experiences is that you need to take your time with children. Things don't always happen instantaneously. You must balance your own disappointment when change does not occur overnight. It takes time for children to become cooperative and considerate, respectful of themselves, and respectful of others, particularly when other forces are pulling them in another direction. It takes time to develop feelings of trust, acceptance, and personal value—more time for some kids than others. Patience, persistence, and optimism eventually lead to success.

One preschool teacher who used some of my cooperative games in this book with her 4-year-olds commented on how she tied the cooperative concept into putting away larger equipment:

> The children have just begun to help put away larger equipment. I started with pushing benches back to the wall. At first they were on both sides, so the bench went in circles. Then one child said, "Everyone on one side and push." It took about 2 to 3 minutes to get it there, but they cheered when they finished. They also now put their own little mats away and are quite good at cooperating.

It is clear that we can enhance children's cooperative perspectives and cooperative skills by designing games and activities with this in mind and by providing more opportunities for children to accomplish different tasks together (such as moving equipment that they cannot move alone). Another powerful medium for nurturing meaningful cooperation at an early age is play equipment that works best and is most fun when children use it together (e.g., cooperative swings, rocking horses, balancing boards, tricycles, pedal cars, trains, slides, and other play equipment built for two or more children). Almost all of our play equipment is designed for only one child (e.g., a traditional swing), but there are cooperative swings and slides with places for eight or more children, and the children have a great time playing together on that equipment. Cooperative equipment is designed to work better and elicit greater feelings of success when children use it together in a cooperative way. At least some of our playground and playroom equipment should function best only when two or more children play together cooperatively with it. This might include more cooperative play props, such as giant potato sacks or giant caterpillar covers, which encourage children to play in a cooperative way for a common objective. These kinds of play materials and play opportunities nurture early cooperation in a very natural way.

When children's play, games, and play equipment are designed with the children's overall development in mind, and adapted specifically for the positive development of young children, we all gain something of value. To move in this direction, encourage children to construct their own creations or equipment together, to move it into place together, and to play with it together. They can move with it, within it, under it, on top of it, or through it, or they can make it move together. Children's self-confidence is also enhanced at an early age when they are provided with balls, bats, boats, nets, hoops, goals, pucks, fields, standards, and playground and gymnastics equipment that is designed with little people's success in mind. The bottom line is to provide ample play materials and games that make it easy and enjoyable for little children to cooperate and more likely for them to succeed.

Parents, teachers, day-care providers, older siblings, and good babysitters are well positioned to introduce cooperative games to children and reinforce positive interaction among children.

Embracing the simple joys together.

Parents, there's one point I'd like to mention that too many parents overlook: Both parents can play with their children and participate in preschool activities with their kids. When you play with children at home or join them in their preschool activities, it is often the highlight of their day. In the cooperative nursery schools and kindergartens in which I've worked, mothers and fathers are encouraged to take the time to volunteer as assistants or to just spend some time with the children in this context on a regular basis. Too few parents take full advantage of these very time-limited opportunities.

I'd like to tell you, dads and moms, that if you are not taking advantage of this opportunity, you are missing out on one of life's most enriching experiences. You will never again have this opportunity to spend time with each of your children at this age and in this context. Watching 3-, 4-, and 5-year-olds finding their own way, engaging fully in play, and sharing their own novel interpretations of life and games gives a pleasure hard to describe. If you put away your work or your thoughts about what you "have to do" today and connect totally with children in their play and in other activities, you will all gain something of value. When you embrace special moments together, your children know and feel in their hearts that you care enough to put other things aside just to be with them. It is extremely important that your child feel fully loved to develop a strong sense of personal worth. This special time together also provides you with a wonderful opportunity to participate more fully in your son's or daughter's one brief childhood. Just remember, the time you spend playing, listening, interacting, and learning with your child is all part of a larger process of nurturing a positive, caring, and productive human being. Children live in this special, magical place and age for a short time, and this time passes quickly. If you fail to seize this opportunity to be with them fully now, it will be gone forever.

Outside of the kindergarten, nursery school, or playschool context, a fine occasion to put some of these cooperative games into play can be at family outings, children's birthday parties, beach days, or picnics. These are, after all, intended to be celebrations of life, not places for fighting and crying—as is too often the case when children play party games that leave some children feeling like losers.

Cooperative Pin the Tail on the Donkey

One inventive mother took the occasion of her 5-year-old son's birthday to adapt the traditional Pin the Tail on the Donkey in a new cooperative way. In her version, children helped each other to accurately pin the tail on the donkey by calling out directions or instructions to the blindfolded person. In another adaptation, they worked together to assemble the entire animal on the wall, each taking turns adding a different body part—leg, head, tail—and again directing the blindfolded person to the proper place on the wall. The results were lots of cheers and absolutely no tears. For younger children, playmates can help their friends find the donkey by physically guiding them in the right direction if they get off track.

Cooperative Hide and Seek

This is another way to enhance cooperation in a well-known game while keeping the fun. In this game, two children (hand in hand) begin as seekers while the rest of the children hide around the house or play area. Each time the seekers find someone, they take her by the hand, and together this larger group of seekers tries to find another hider. It takes a lot of cooperation to get everyone going in the same direction, but as one mother commented, "the results were worth the effort." Cooperative Hide and Seek can also be played with players hiding in pairs and seeking in pairs. It is often more fun for young children to hide together and seek together. Occasionally we have asked a whole group of children to search for a pair of children (or adults) who are hiding or "lost in the bush" (even if the bush happens to be behind a door or under a bed).

Children Teaching Children

Most children love to teach other children or show other people (large or small) how to do new things. We can take advantage of this eagerness by encouraging young children to teach or help others learn almost anything of value (e.g., how to play a cooperative game, be nice to others, perform a new skill, write letters or names, draw a picture, use a computer, or relax themselves). We encourage small teams of children to work together to teach cooperative games to other children. They can come up with their own plan on how they will teach their game, then go ahead and teach it.

To turn the teaching process into a cooperative game, we sometimes give each child on the team one piece of the game-teaching puzzle. For example, if a game has three simple rules, each member of the team of three children would be given one rule of the game, and they would each be responsible for teaching that rule. Another option for teaching a new cooperative game is to create picture cards for how the game is played. Each child is given a picture depicting one part of the game. The three children then get together in a group, and each child explains his specific rule so that all three children can then play the game. Or the teaching children can simply show the other children how to play the game by each playing a role in a real demonstration.

5

Remaking Adult Games

Many of the cooperative games previously discussed in this book, particularly the collective-score games, can be played successfully and enjoyed by teenagers and adults, as long as the game is kept appropriately challenging for the group. Some teens and adults will prefer cooperative games; others will prefer games that are competitive. This chapter focuses on how to keep the fun and cooperation in games that are more competitive in structure.

Very few people enjoy losing or feeling like a loser or a failure. Therefore the challenge for keeping the fun in competitive games lies in finding joy—or highlights—in each game and keeping the outcome of the game in perspective. The majority of people in the world who play games do so to enhance the quality of their day or to add joyfulness to their lives in some small way. They want to have fun; add some challenge, excitement, or intensity to their day; and share positive experiences with others.

Very few people who play games are, or ever become, high-performance athletes or professional athletes, where outcomes really count.

Sometimes when playing games, it helps to remind ourselves and others of why we participate. What really matters in a game is that we become fully engaged in it and find some joy or lift within it. The challenge is to live our lives and play our games with a sense of perspective. In the big picture, the outcome of the game doesn't really matter. What matters is the outcome of the person. What really matters is that we find meaning and joy in our lives and that we find ways to lift the lives of our loved ones.

Whether you are playing cards, table games, cooperative games, or competitive sports, it is important to focus on the process of playing and enjoy the good parts of the experience. Problems surface for you and others when too much emphasis is placed on the score, the win or loss outcome. How much attention do you place on the result? How far will you go in order to win? How do you feel and react when you lose? Can you lose and still leave feeling better for having embraced the experience? Can you find good things to remember and lessons to embrace regardless of the outcome? If yes, then you are playing with perspective. If not, then you would probably gain from playing with more perspective and placing less emphasis on the result.

The noblest objective for most people playing games (young or old) is to come together to play in a happy, healthy, fun-filled context. Even

Everyone can embrace the pure joy of play in many different contexts.

when there is competition, there is also cooperation as teammates play together, help each other, and include everyone. I often refer to these kinds of activities as semicooperative games because everyone is included and the players on both teams remain infinitely more important than the outcome of the game. The overriding goal is for everyone to leave the game feeling somehow enriched by the experience. This is a realistic possibility, even within competitive structures, but only if the right perspective and spirit are brought into the game. One's perspective on winning or losing and one's perception of the importance of scoreboard winning or losing are the important factors, not the win or loss itself. In the end, those who keep the game in perspective and enjoy the game most are the real winners.

We can help children, teenagers, and adults keep the joy in the pursuit by reminding them to play for the love of the game, to look for the simple joys in each experience, to think about their highlights from each game, and to reflect on how they can continue to enjoy participating in the activity or playing the game.

ADAPTING GAMES FOR JOY AND INCLUSION

Examples of how some games and intramural sports have been adapted to keep teenagers, adults, and senior citizens joyfully involved are presented here. Play with some of these ideas to see if you can integrate or adapt any of them into your games. Ask your players to come up with their own ideas for ensuring that all the players get the most fun out of their playing experiences.

In slow-pitch softball, the pitcher pitches slowly to her own teammates, who have unlimited pitches to hit the ball. Every batter hits every inning. In volleyball, we don't worry about rules such as carrying the ball, touching the net, and hitting the ball twice in a row. In seven-on-a-side touch football, forward passes are allowed from any point, at any time, and every player is an eligible receiver. In inner-tube water polo, people who are not strong swimmers can still play because everyone sits in inner tubes. When the emphasis is placed on fun and activity for all the players, the result is usually more participation and more fun for everyone.

Other game adaptations include the following:

- Play soccer, softball, and touch football without lines. The players often find these games more enjoyable than the "play in a box" versions.
- Bucketball is a modified form of basketball with moving baskets. Team members attempt to score on their own goalie at the other end of the court, who has a wastebasket or wicker basket (bucket)

in his hands. The goalie stands on the floor or a slightly raised platform and helps his teammates score by moving the bucket in the direction of their shots.

- Try novel activities such as the 50-yard (46-meter) crawl; the shot roll; the 120-yard (110-meter) under hurdle; the low jump (a clean leap under a bar that is lowered after each jump); an underwater jacks tournament; games played on stilts; games played on large inner tubes; and games played in rain, snow, sand, or mud.
- In recreational Collective-Score Basketball, the total score for both teams is the focus. Players call their own fouls and turnovers. There is free substitution on the run (with no stoppage in play), no foul shooting or jump balls, and no record of team standings. Firsthand observation and feedback from the participants indicate a full-inclusion situation that "operates at a faster pace—thus providing more physical exercise—promotes cooperation of both teams toward a mutual goal, fosters development of positive social interaction, and provides an environment where ability is not the prime consideration for who does or does not play."

It's interesting to see what happens once people are provided with a choice. In speaking about one alternative program the coordinator said,

> If one team doesn't have enough players, the other team will share. If you want to play with seven to a side in volleyball, then play with seven. There's no reason for people having to stand on the sidelines. Nobody worries about gaining a playoff spot because there are no playoffs. Nobody cares about getting two points if you win a game. Perhaps most gratifying of all is to actually see adults having fun. Watching them laughing and joking while playing is like night and day compared to competitive sports.

The future is right now, putting your ideas and the ideas of your players to the test in the real world. You never know what works unless you try . . . so let's try to move forward collectively by putting our ideas on the line.

In addition to playing down the importance of scoreboard winning, you can use other concrete strategies in different types of game structures to bring everyone into the action, to equalize teams, to rotate positions, to provide successful experiences, and to nurture cooperation. If you closely observe a game such as indoor soccer, you will discover that some players never touch the ball. How can they feel included? One cooperative strategy I introduced to alleviate this problem with children is called "all touch." Before a shot is taken, the ball must be passed to and touched by all members of the team. A similar strategy can be implemented in scoring. In "all score," all the players must score a goal before a team can win. Before long, players begin to include all their teammates in the action spontaneously even when such "rules" are no longer in effect. We usually use oversized goals (or no goalies) for additional fun when playing "all score" in sports such as soccer or floor hockey.

In floor hockey or ball hockey, all walls are in play. There are no officials, no offsides, and no face-offs; consequently there is very little stoppage in play. A certain time is slotted for each game. Within this time period the captains, together with their teams, determine the start and end of the game as well as the length of halftime. If desired, all the available time can be spent playing.

A high school basketball coach enrolled in one of my courses suggested a scoring modification to increase cooperation among team members and to avoid situations where one player scores most (or all) of the points: Subtract the difference between the high and low scorers' point totals from their team's total score. For example, let's assume one team scored 30 points, with their high scorer netting 10 points and their low scorer getting 0 points. The team's final score would be 20 (30 minus 10), or the total score minus the difference between high and low scorers. If the other team scored 24 points, with the high scorer getting 6 points and the low scorer getting 2, their final score would also be 20 points (24 minus 4).

Another option is to give bonus points to a team for every team member who scores (e.g., 2 bonus points awarded for each player on the team who scores) or a lump sum bonus of 15 points if all team members score. This provides incentive to give everybody a chance to play and score and encourages the development of cooperative and exciting game tactics.

Try introducing rotational strategies, either within one team or between two teams. For within-team rotation, the players simply rotate through the various offensive and defensive positions during the course of the game so that everyone gets a chance to play every position. This prevents players from being allocated to one position, as in "You play outfield," or "You play goalie," or "You block" for the rest of their "playing" lives. For between-team rotation, the rotational process extends to the other team. It can be done in virtually any sport. In Rotational Volleyball, for example, the server rotates to the other team. This allows players to focus on the process of playing in the "here and now" regardless of which position they are playing or which side of the net they are on. In addition, it helps keep the game in perspective. How can you get angry at the other team or lose to the other team when you are, or will become, the other team at some point in the game?

Some teams choose to reserve between-team trades for situations where teams are obviously not balanced in terms of skill level. Lopsided scores don't usually provide the best kind of challenge for anyone. It's better to give the other team an extra player or two, or to switch a few players during the course of the game, to even things up and keep the challenge optimal. The ultimate objective here is to have teams so evenly matched that they play a close, exciting game or play to a tie. In some sports, uneven teams can also be evened up without making player exchanges. One way of doing this is to make adjustments in the size of the goal, court, or net. For example, larger buckets, lower buckets, or more hoops could be placed at one end of the court (for modified basketball), or a longer bench could serve as the goal at one end of the field and a shorter one at the other end for games such as soccer.

Another strategy involves the rotation of players during the course of a tournament rather than during the course of a game. This approach was tried in a hockey tournament for house-league players. Players from different teams and different areas got to play together on different teams during the course of the tournament. Social interaction, making new friends, and working together with new teammates became the focal point.

A citywide rotational gymnastics meet used a slightly different tack to create relatively equal teams. Gymnasts from different schools and clubs were placed on teams based on their coaches' assessments of their abilities. Former competitors helped and cheered their newfound teammates. New bonds were formed, particularly between very young gymnasts and their older counterparts. This same principle was successfully applied in an upper elementary interschool sports program. All students interested in participating were placed on a team, with an attempt made to equalize teams from various areas of the city. Friendships were often built between schools by having half of a team's members originate from one school and half originate from another. Other definite pluses of the program include that no players were "cut," everybody was given equal playing time during games, teams were kept small to ensure adequate playing time for each person, and no compilation of records or scores was kept. Because the scoreboard "stakes" weren't so high and because teams were mixed, a relaxed and healthy atmosphere permeated most games.

It would be interesting to try this approach at an international level to really bring athletes from different countries together, to move beyond the competition and enhance mutual cooperation and mutual understanding. An alternative structure for at least some parts of Olympic or other high-level international (or even university) competitions would be to include volleyball, basketball, ice hockey, field hockey, baseball, or track or swimming relay teams made up of players from different countries. When national teams tour other countries for friendly competition, why not play at least some games with team members from both sides?

COOPERATIVE GIFTS

One of the most cooperative and valued gifts you can give your loved ones—wife, husband, boyfriend, girlfriend, children, family—is the gift of your time. Here is a specific gift idea. Write a note to your wife, husband, or other important loved one outlining your special gift: My gift to you and me is to meet once a week at a specific time (with no distractions) solely to talk about how we can keep the joy in our relationship and rekindle the joy in each of our own lives or to do something that we enjoy doing together. Then set the time, write it down on the calendar, and stick to it because it is potentially the most important meeting of your life. If occasionally one of you is out of town on that date, then reschedule before you leave, and mark it on your calendar with a star.

A cooperative gift of time together with your child or children might be to play with them with no distractions or do something with them that they like to do and choose to do at least once a week. This is a time for you to connect with your child or children in a joyful or playful way when you are fully there and not thinking about other things. Commit yourself to just be there with them fully, follow their lead, and embrace your special time together.

6

Cooperative Games From Other Cultures

The more I have studied and learned firsthand about earlier cultures and their play, the more I realize how narrow our contemporary view of play and games has become. Clearly our contemporary view of games and sport is not the view held by aboriginal people who first inhabited most of this planet. I am sharing the following examples of cooperative games from other cultures in hopes of broadening our collective horizon of what games can be. Let your thoughts wander. Reflect on the concepts behind the games and how these concepts may be related to living in harmony. Str-e-e-e-tch your mind. See if you can come up with your own adaptations for some of these games. See if you can enhance some of the games you now play in your own home, day care, school, gym, camp, or playground.

In many original games played by aboriginal people, teams developed spontaneously, changed readily, or were chosen in ways that ensured all players felt included. One idea I particularly like is how the North American Indians saved face when choosing teams or sides for games. Each player threw his hat or glove or stick in a pile. One player who was blindfolded or who closed his eyes then picked up the sticks and threw one to his right and one to his left until all the sticks were distributed. Those were the teams. No players were humiliated or forced to wait anxiously, dreading the possibility of not being chosen or being chosen last. This way of choosing sides began long ago when the village chief sat inside a circle at the center of the playing field. All the players' sticks (e.g., when playing the game of lacrosse) were placed in a heap in front of him. After being blindfolded, he picked sticks two at a time and placed one on his right and one on his left until all the sticks were gone. Players then ran to the two piles of sticks, found their own, and joined that team. Another respectful method used for choosing teams was for the chief or leader to place strips of two different colors of tree bark or paper in a small pouch or covered basket. Each player drew out one slip of paper and was designated to a team based on the color chosen.

Think about the lessons you can draw from the different approaches discussed in this chapter. This is why I have chosen to share them with you.

GAMES FROM ABORIGINAL CULTURES

Play and games are an integral part of the daily lives of aboriginal people. When I refer to aboriginal people, I am speaking primarily of the original

Young women from Papua New Guinea joyfully engage in cooperative games.

people who have lived on the land and very close to nature for many, many centuries (e.g., the Inuit and Eskimo people who inhabit the Arctic regions of North America, the Indian and Dene people who live in many regions of North America, the Australian Aboriginal people, and diverse groups of people who live in small jungle villages throughout Papua New Guinea).

Aboriginal Winning Marbles

This marble game played by Australian Aboriginal children has an interesting twist. Two players sit facing each other cross-legged, about 10 feet (3 meters) apart. Each player has a small cluster of marbles on the ground directly in front of him. The players take turns attempting to hit the other person's marbles by rolling one of their own marbles in that direction. When a shot is successful, the marbles that are hit are placed in front of the successful shooter along with his other marbles. If the shot is not successful, the rolled marble remains wherever it stops. As a result, this game can go back and forth indefinitely because as one player's cluster of marbles diminishes in size, it becomes harder to hit; as the other player's cluster of marbles increases in size, it becomes easier to hit because there are so many marbles in the cluster.

Collective Pin

This cooperative bowling game was played by a remote group of Indian children in Guatemala. A wooden pin is set up at a moderate distance from a throwing line. The players decide how far away to put the pin. The objective of the game is for children to work together to get the first ball rolled (the lead ball) to touch a wooden pin without knocking the pin over. All players are on the same team. After the first player rolls her ball (the lead ball) toward the pin, each subsequent player rolls her ball in an attempt to nudge the lead ball closer to the pin. The game is won when the lead ball touches the pin, without knocking it over. If the pin is knocked over, the player who knocked it over starts a new game by rolling the first ball.

GAMES FROM NEW GUINEA AND PAPUA NEW GUINEA

The Hanahan culture of Papua New Guinea has no word for "winning" in its traditional language, which is almost inconceivable from our current view of the world. If a person does something well, it is acknowledged that he is good at these skills. The important thing is for everyone to participate, to develop their skills, and to help each other get better at whatever they are doing. Part of their underlying philosophy is that no child ever be excluded from a group.

The following cooperative games are played by peaceful and cooperative people in New Guinea and Papua New Guinea.

Manumanu (Little Bird)

One child stands on a long, sturdy wooden plank, which is raised a foot or two off the ground and carried around by her teammates. While holding a stick as a balancing rod, she sings and dances on the moving plank. The goal for all children is to keep the child safely balanced on the plank as they carry it. The children take turns being the little bird and helping keep the manumanu in flight.

Evanena (Walking Down the Pole)

Two rows of children face each other and make a platform of linked arms. One boy stands up on the arms of the first two in line and walks forward across the joined arms of the others to the end of the line. As he moves along the platform of linked arms, those who are no longer supporting him run to the other end of the line, extending the platform as the walker moves forward. In many of the group games of the Motu people, when one group (or individual) achieves the goal, the players merely change places to give the other group (or individual) a chance to achieve the goal.

When I was studying the play and games of cooperative aboriginal people in Papua New Guinea, I discovered and personally observed some games that had the ultimate goal of ending in a tie (or an equal score). I was living in a small jungle village in the Konga area of the North Solomon Islands of Papua New Guinea, specifically to learn about their traditional cooperative play and games. I was both surprised and intrigued when I learned about the following tie game and the concept behind it. For those raised in North America or most technologically advanced countries, it is a very unique concept that the goal of a game be to end in a tie score.

The game is called Makii, and it is played by two teams with spinning tops. There are a number of different versions of this game, but the simplest way to play is as follows.

Makii

The players form two teams. A number of coconuts are spread out on the ground in front of the teams (the number of coconuts and distance away from the players are decided by the two teams). Each player on one team takes a turn throwing a homemade spinning top at the coconut targets. If a target is hit, it is removed from the playing area. After everyone on the first team has a turn, these coconut targets are put back. The players on the second team then take turns throwing tops. Their goal is to hit the same number of coconut targets as the first team. This presents a unique challenge for the second team, both when the first team hit lots of targets and when they did not hit many targets. For example, if the first few players on the second team tie the first team's score and there are still a couple of players left to throw, those players must throw their tops into the field of targets without hitting any. They are not allowed to throw them off to the side, away from the playing field.

Another more complex game designed to end in a tie is played by the Tangu people of New Guinea. The only way to win this game, called Taketak, is to tie (i.e., each team must have the same score at the end of the game). The game represents the dominant theme of moral equality in Tangu culture.

Taketak

The name *Taketak* comes from the Tangu word for the hard spines of coconut fronds or leaves. To play the game, these spines (or taketaks) are stripped of their soft leafy part and struck into the ground in two play areas, or lots, separated by about 5 yards or meters. Each lot contains approximately 30 taketaks. Hollow homemade spinning tops, 2 to 3 inches (5 to 8 centimeters) in diameter, are made by forcing a wooden spindle through the center of a dried jungle fruit. Players throw these spinning tops at the taketaks. The taketaks themselves are staked into the ground about 6 inches (15 centimeters) apart in a manner that ensures they do not form parallel or diagonal lines, which would allow tops to be thrown down empty corridors.

The players form two teams, each of which has the same number of tops and approximately the same number of players. To start the game, one player spins his top in the palm of his hand and, in one motion, throws it into one of the lots of taketaks, trying to hit as many as possible. Any taketaks that are touched while the top is either in flight or spinning on the ground are pulled out and laid aside. Once all the players from both teams have thrown their tops into their respective lots, round 1 is over. Unless the score is equal at that point, one of the two teams replaces a couple of taketaks in its lot, and both teams go through a second round in the same manner as the first.

Let's suppose the first team struck three taketaks (and therefore removed three taketaks) in the first round, and the second team struck (and removed) two. The first team replaces two taketaks in its lot. Now team 1 has one taketak removed, and team 2 has two removed. In the second round, if the first team hits one taketak, it is removed, leaving both teams with two taketaks out of their lots. Both teams are now equivalent as to the number of taketaks removed, but the players from team 2 still need to take their second round of shots. Their objective is now to throw their tops into their lot without hitting any taketaks. If their tops are thrown fairly into the middle of their lot and they succeed in not hitting any, both teams are declared winners (equivalent). If on the other hand the second team hits one taketak, they have now removed three and are not yet equivalent. Since the round is over and the score is not tied, team 2 replaces two taketaks. The game continues in this manner until a draw is reached or until the players tire, agree that they are equal, and suspend the game. Tying requires the refined skill (and good fortune) of being able to hit taketaks when necessary and miss them when necessary.

A game designed to end in a tie is intriguing in itself and opens up many new possibilities. Continual replacement (in this case, of taketaks) is also an important concept that allows the game to continue until an equal score is reached or until there is mutual agreement that it is time to stop. Replacement may occur in several ways. Perhaps the simplest way is for the teams to take turns replacing two taketaks after each round of play. Another possibility, which serves to keep teams and scores relatively equal, is for the team that has the most taketaks removed after each round of play to replace two taketaks. Still another possibility is for the team that has the most taketaks removed after each round to replace the total number of taketaks that the other team has removed. For example, team 1 has removed seven and team 2 has removed three; team 1 therefore replaces three taketaks into its lot. Finally, we could consider the possibility of having the higher-scoring team replace the number of taketaks that represents the difference between the two teams. For example, team 1 has removed seven and team 2 has removed three; team 1 therefore replaces four taketaks, and another full round begins. Many potential scoring systems can be explored in regard to replacement and equivalence.

When playing games of this nature with children in your own schools or communities, keep the rules simple and let the children help you adapt the games so they work best—keeping in mind that the goal is to end in a tie and to have fun and be challenged in the process.

The concept of playing to a tie is not restricted to the Tangu people. The Asmat people of New Guinea used to race dugout canoes across a river but always reached the other side at the same instant. When soccer was first introduced to their children, they played to a tie. When Inuit youth in the Canadian Arctic began cross-country skiing, they skied hard but tried to cross the finish line at the same instant, and Australian Aboriginal children often ran to a tie. When I was out running trails with a friend one day, I decided to try to run to a tie without telling him. It was fun because you're never quite sure of the other's strategy. You run hard and he runs hard; he slows down and you slow down. The last 50 yards or meters, when you are usually clipping along at a healthy pace, is all anticipation. How are we going to hit the line at the same instant? Then . . . victory!

INUIT GAMES FROM THE CANADIAN ARCTIC

Some of the most joyful and cooperative games I have ever seen were played by Inuit children in the Canadian Arctic. I visited remote Inuit settlements in the Canadian north over a period of many years in the early 1970s and was always uplifted by the open and playful spirit of the children.*

Muk (Silence)

This game centers around laughter. Players begin by sitting in a circle. One player moves into the middle of the circle. She then chooses another player, who must say, "Muk" (silence), and then remain silent and straight-faced. The person in the middle uses comical expressions and gestures to try to "break the muk." The player to break the muk is dubbed with a comical name and replaces the person in the middle. Another version of this game is for the person in the middle of the circle to try to make anyone in the circle laugh. If successful, the person who laughed goes to the middle of the circle, and the game continues.

---

*I helped put together a film that shows some Inuit and Indian games called *Northern Games* (1981). It's available from the National Film Board of Canada, www.nfb.ca, 800-267-7710.

Eskimo Winning Marbles

In the Bering coast of Alaska, the Eskimo children played one version of marbles without losers almost daily in the summer months. In this game, each child brings one marble to the game, plays with it, and leaves the game with the same marble. Small groups of children come together to enjoy themselves and to embrace the challenge of hitting the scattered marbles. Their traditional game of marbles has no provisions for winning another player's marble. Their belief is that there is simply no need to walk off with another child's marble in order to be challenged or to have fun. In fact, when the "winner and loser" version of marbles, which is the only one most of us know, was first introduced, the children felt it took away from the fun and chose not to play it.

Blanket Toss

Originally a large durable blanket was made by sewing together several walrus hides. The blanket was about 10 to 12 feet (3 to 3 1/2 meters) wide. One player would sit or stand in the middle of the blanket, and a group of 20 to 30 players would spread out around the blanket and catapult the middle person high in the air. The blankets used today are large circular canvas structures with a heavy rope intertwined around the edge for a secure grip. This forms something like a very large trampoline, propelled by the power of the people cooperating around the edge. The cooperative challenge is to not only toss the person high in the air (preferably straight up) but also catch the person safely when she comes back down.

Nuglutang

This popular game of sharing is played particularly during the months of darkness. A spindle-shaped piece of caribou antler with a hole drilled through it is hung above the players' heads so that it dangles at about shoulder height. The players stand around the target holding pointed rods, something similar to large pencils but made out of bone and rounded at the tip. Each person tries to slip the tip of her rod into the hole in the target (while it is moving), all at the same time. This sets the target swinging all over the place. The first person to place his rod in the target is the "winner"; he puts up as a stake anything he wishes that has value, such as a harpoon head or knife, and retires from the play. The second winner assumes ownership of the first stake but in turn replaces it with another. The game continues this way until the lone last player manages to hit the target. Because the game is then finished, he does not have to replace the stake. Thus the only person to "lose" anything (in our terms) is the first "winner," and the only one to win anything, without having to give something back in return, is the last "winner" (loser?). From their perspective, there was honor and meaning in giving, so those who give are the real winners. This game is played amid peals of laughter, and many excess goods are exchanged.

Kaipsak (Spinning Tops)

This is a favorite among Inuit children. Each child, in turn, spins a top and then races out of the icehouse (igloo), runs around it, and tries to get back in before the top stops spinning. In another spinning game, children sometimes become the tops themselves by sitting on a block of ice and being spun around by the other children until they say, "Stop," or became too dizzy to stay in the seat. The next "rider" then takes a turn. The children occasionally hook up one of their sledge dogs to a block of ice or pair of skis and go for a whirl. Lots of fun.

Airplane Carry

In what used to be called the Spread Eagle Carry, now referred to as the Airplane Carry, one person lies facedown on the ground, with arms stretched out straight to the sides. Three carriers pick him up, one child by each wrist (or near each elbow for children) and one by both ankles. Once they lift the "eagle" off the ground, they carry him as far as possible

before he collapses. The eagle is carried slowly, usually about a foot or two off the ground, and lowered gently as he begins to collapse. In this game, all of the birds smile before taking off, and most of them smile after landing. Crash landings can sometimes momentarily interrupt bird smiles but do not seem to inhibit laughter from the rest of the flock.

Dog Sledge

Samuel King Hutton, an early Arctic explorer, wrote in his personal logbook (a chronological diary of his adventure to the Arctic) about the sheer joy and excitement he witnessed when watching Inuit children playing:

> For sheer merriment there is nothing to beat the sledge game without dogs, when six or seven of the boys slip the harness on their own shoulders and race away with the sledge, wheeling this way and that at the command of their driver. They enter most heartily into the fun, crossing from one place to another in the team, just as dogs do, snapping and yelping and whining and tugging to be on the move every time the driver calls a halt.

A similar kind of game can be played on snow with toboggans, plastic snow sleds, cross-country skis, or inflated inner tubes or on a floating mattress in shallow water. A variation can be played in a gym or on a hardwood floor using scooters or a four-wheeled dolly and a rope. One child (the driver) sits or kneels on the sledge (dolly), and three or four others grasp the rope, thereby becoming sledge dogs. To slow the game down to a walk or safe trot, the dogs can be informed that they can walk fast but cannot run because they cannot lose the driver who will guide them and feed them. The driver directs the dogs through a course (around a series of marker cones). For younger children, this same concept can be tied into Christmas activities with Santa and his reindeer.

CHINESE NURSERY SCHOOL GAMES

When visiting and conducting research in nursery schools and kindergartens in China (in the 1970s), I observed young children playing these cooperative games.

Helping Grow the Flowers

In this cooperative role-playing game, preschool children act out different ways each child could help in the process of growing and harvesting flowers. Teams are made up of six children; each team of six has a hoe, some cardboard or plastic flowers, a watering can, a manure bucket, a spray can, a wicker basket, and a tricycle. The equipment is placed at the far end of the play area, and the teams line up at the other end. To begin the game, the first child on each team runs down to his team's equipment at the far end of the play area, picks up the hoe, hoes the ground to prepare the earth for planting (about five strokes), then runs back to his team. The second child runs down and plants the flowers (cardboard or plastic flowers), then runs back to her team. The third child then runs down to water the flowers with the watering can before running back. The fourth child runs down to the manure bucket, spreads the fertilizer, then runs back to his team. The fifth child runs down and sprays the flowers with natural fertilizer to protect them before running back to her team. The sixth child runs down, harvests the flowers, puts them in the wicker basket, hops on the tricycle, and rides back to her team, taking the flowers to market.

Big Turnip

In this role-playing game, children act out helping each other harvest a turnip. One child squats down, pretending to be a huge turnip growing in the ground. (When I saw this game being played, the child wore a costume that resembled a huge turnip.) The children are told that a single child cannot pull him out of the ground ("pick him") because the turnip is so large. A predetermined number of children helping each other is needed before the turnip can be pulled out of the ground. Although it's lots of fun, the larger objective of this game is for children to learn that you can accomplish some things working together that you cannot accomplish alone.

SoFa Circle Game

The children are divided into two equal groups. Half the children form a large outer circle around the other half of the children (who form an inner circle). The children in the outer circle begin to sing a song and clap their hands to the rhythm of the song. The children in the inner circle skip around inside the circle clapping their hands. When the children sing a specific word in the song—*SoFa*—each child inside the circle stops in front of someone in the outer circle, and together they play a quick pat-a-cake game while singing a rhythmic tune. They then clap their hands together, spin around quickly, shake hands with the child in front of them, and change places.

7 Creating Your Own Games and Evaluating Your Success

It is through creating and sharing positive play and games that we will ultimately come up with our most enjoyable and beneficial games. When trying to invent new and better games for children, remember that the framework of the game is vitally important. In the designing process, think about what kind of response the game is likely to elicit or demand. Will everyone be fully included in the action? Will anyone be left out or feel left out? Will everyone have fun and leave happier than when they began? To what extent will they all feel like winners or feel as if they won something of value? Is respectful cooperation one of the underlying guiding lights?

The attitude or perspective taken into a game, and reinforced within the game, is also extremely important, especially in more challenging or competitive pursuits. If there is an element of competition, is it respectful competition? Does the game context teach children to be respectful of themselves and others? Is the game joyful? Does it provide children with opportunities for positive interaction with each other? Is the game appropriately challenging for the age group? Is it centered on personal growth, respect for others, and ongoing learning? Does the play experience allow children to develop in positive ways—physically, socially, psychologically, and emotionally?

There is a tendency for some children and many adults to create games within the framework they are most familiar with, probably because this is what they know best. This may mean that for many people, competition against others will be their guiding force. Therefore it is helpful to discuss the goals of cooperative games and let the group play some enjoyable cooperative games before they engage in the game-creation process. This can help the creation process flourish in a more cooperative and constructive direction.

It is interesting to note that over a number of years, when I have given children opportunities to freely create their own "fun" games, they have never created games where they hit or smash into each other, where large numbers of children remain stationary or inactive (sitting on a bench or standing on the sidelines waiting for their turn), or where children are eliminated from play. Hitting each other, waiting inactively for a turn, and eliminating players are adult concepts and not what children initially create or choose on their own.

We have found that the younger the child, or the less conditioning a person has had to the necessity of always competing against others, the more humane the game is likely to be. Even 4- and 5-year-olds can come up with some beautifully cooperative activities when they use their wonderful imaginations. During a "potato party," a group of kindergarten children created the game of Mashed Potato. One child was the "potato," and the other children were the "milk." The milk was poured in one child at a time to stick to the potato. This pouring of milk was accomplished only with the child's imagination and a few pouring gestures. When they were all "stuck" together in the group, they spontaneously jumped around, still stuck together, to make a whole pot of mashed potatoes.

The children invented the game completely on their own. A 5-year-old girl was the leader, with ideas coming from several others. On another occasion a group of 4-year-olds invented a hoop-dragging game, in which the children took turns pulling each other around on their bellies with a hula hoop. Our experiences have demonstrated that children are never too young for constructive creative input. We just have to give them the chance.

In one attempt at creating new games, I gave a group of fourth- and fifth-grade students 30 minutes to try to make up some new games or

Young children can create joyful, imaginative games.

change old ones to make them more fun. I began by telling them what I was trying to do with my games: to have everyone participate and help one another, to let everyone have fun, and to have no one feeling like a loser. I gave a few examples of cooperative games that they had already played (Log Roll, Collective-Score Volleyball, Collective Rounders) and told them they could use any equipment they wanted for their games. I asked them to split into groups of three or four, and away they went.

The creation process was beautiful to sit in on. Lots of creative ideas were flowing as the kids developed their games. Children were working together, interacting verbally, and sharing and refining ideas. When we went to the gym, each group had an opportunity to try out their game with their own little group in order to make any refinements necessary before teaching it to the class. For the next three gym classes, the kids taught their games to their classmates. After each game, we had a brief discussion to get their comments on the game and suggestions for improvement. The students were later given an opportunity to present and assess their refined game in another class. Two games were generally presented at the same time in different halves of the gym to keep the groups small.

Cooperative interaction was clearly apparent in the creation of the games, in the teaching of the games by the kids, in the playing of the games, in the evaluation of the games, and in the suggestions for improvement. When given the opportunity, the children came up with some very good games on very short notice. It was obvious from this game-creation process that the children understood the importance of participation, fun, and cooperation.

Marie Riley and Kate Barrett were among the first people I heard from who had involved themselves extensively in implementing what children have to offer in the way of game creation. Their child-designed games evolved primarily from classes of 9-, 10-, and 11-year-olds who had previously been exposed to a cooperative games climate that allowed them to work at their own rate and to feel free to make mistakes.

When I watched some of these children playing their own game creations, it was immediately apparent that there was no competition against others, no putting others down, no elimination of players, and rarely any set boundary lines. The ball games they created involved lots of activity and a great deal of contact with the ball by all children. In one game (designed to include some element of striking), two children hit a ball back and forth over a net using many different body parts. The net was attached to the backs of two chairs. One of the children was highly skilled and could have easily drilled the ball past his partner. When asked why he did not do that he said, "Then there would be no game." Besides, he added, they were both "playing against the net."

Junior and senior high school students are just as capable of inventing creative cooperative games as younger children. I had the opportunity to speak to approximately 100 junior and senior high school students who were involved in conducting intramural programs in their own schools. This conference had been organized and conducted by students for fellow students who were interested in improving their intramural programs. Together we enjoyed an afternoon of Collective-Score Blanketball, Collective Monsterball Volleyball, Collective Orbit, Bump and Scoot, Crossover Dodgeball, and All-Touch Scooter Ball.

After we played together, I asked the students to divide into small groups to discuss their feelings about the cooperative games they had just played and to attempt to create some of their own alternatives. The students generated many interesting comments and good suggestions for new or modified games. One group wrote, "The more different or ridiculous a game is, the less competitive it is likely to be." For example, when floor hockey is played with a beach ball; basketball is played with a monsterball; or touch football is played with a pumpkin, watermelon, or water balloon, the fun takes priority over the competition. Another group stated, "Teachers and students playing cooperative games or collective sports together would promote better spirit, and more people would feel inclined to try it. A better relationship between people would be developed."

Don Morris, one of the first people who looked to high school students for new game ideas, found teenagers' input to be extremely valuable.

When he asked a group of ninth-grade students to design a game that accounted for the different abilities of each student in the class, they came up with a modified version of softball in which seven bases were set up in a figure-eight pattern. Each batter could choose from a variety of different-sized balls and bats, as well as how the pitcher would deliver the ball. The more highly skilled players chose to use a regulation bat and softball thrown in the traditional manner, while some lesser-skilled students chose to have a large rubber ball rolled toward them and to strike it with an oversized, underweight bat. As in traditional softball, the batter had to hit the ball before leaving home plate and had to touch each base without being tagged out before returning home. However, each batter was allowed to stay at bat until the ball was hit forward and could then run to any base, at any time and in any order. Sometimes three people ended up on one base at one time.

In another game called Basketbowl, players were allowed to choose how they would contribute team points. They could opt to bowl the ball to a certain area, throw it through a hula hoop, or shoot it into a basketball net.

Edward Devereux was a longtime proponent of child-directed games, especially those that were created neither by nor specifically for children. His observations of children's pickup games led him to the following conclusions:

> When you watch a bunch of kids playing a self-organized game of sandlot baseball, it is clear that the emphasis is more on having fun than on winning. If the teams are out of balance, they see no problem in shifting one of the stronger players to the other team, right in the middle of the game. They pitch a bit more gently to the littler kids, so they can have some fun too; besides, since numbers are important, you really need them in the game. Errors are met with laughter and teasing more than with anger and derisive comment. As one kid remarked, "In our game, if everyone is tripping over everybody, it's just funny, but in the Little League the coaches get really mad because it's an important game." If the day is becoming too hot, or if the game has begun to lose the interest of the players, there's no problem in calling it quits and moving on to some other activity.*

Many of my personal experiences with young children and youth have convinced me that we can gain greatly by drawing more fully on their

---

*Edward Devereux, *Two Ball Games* (film), 1975, Ithaca, NY: Cornell University, http://rmc.library.cornell.edu/EAD/htmldocs/RMAO3191.html.

creative power. With a few simple guidelines, children and youth can often think in positive and creative ways. I find this very refreshing because their way of thinking seems to have been conditioned out, drained, or has simply faded away in many adult lives. Children have the capacity to contribute so much more than most people realize, toward their own learning and development and toward the betterment of our society. Why not give them the opportunity to do so? Why not challenge them to come up with positive alternatives to enhance all areas of their lives? Why not let them help us and our world to move and flourish in a more life-enhancing direction?

SAMPLE GAMES

I have chosen 12 sample games that were created by children and teenagers I worked with in a school context. The first 7 games (children's games) were created by a group of 9- and 10-year-olds during a half-hour session. The next 5 games (teenagers' games) were created by a group of teenagers during another half-hour session.

Games for Children 12 and Younger

Action

Two lines start side by side, much as in a normal relay. However, the children at the front of each line work together to complete the course as partners. When the first pair arrives at the third station, the next pair starts. The action course consists of six stations, where partners

- bounce a large ball back and forth 4 times;
- jump rope together 10 times;
- throw a small ball back and forth using a large scoop 4 times;
- walk toward each other from opposite ends of a low balance beam, hold on to each other to turn around, and walk back;
- bounce a ball back and forth four times; and
- do a front roll on a mat, side by side.

After completing the actions outlined above, the partners run directly back through the action course, and finish up by jumping into the air together.

It is interesting to note that when returning to the start of the action course, the children come directly through the action rather than go around it. This added some excitement to the game. The normal adult structure would be to have the children return on the outside, away from where the other children are coming down the course.

Find Your Animal

Each person gets a card with the name of a different animal on it, which is kept a secret. A list is then read aloud that tells what animal each other animal must find. The list is circular: for example, the elephant is looking for the lion, the lion for the wolf, the wolf for the dog, the dog for the cat, the cat for the mouse, and the mouse for the elephant. Without making any sounds, each person acts out the animal that is written on the card and attempts to find the animal he is looking for. If a player thinks she's found the right animal, she taps him on the head or shoulder, and that animal must show his card. If it's the right animal, then she holds on to him while he tries to find his animal. In the end there should be a single circle with all the animals holding on to each other.

To add some additional challenge, the game creators made up decoy cards. One decoy card is distributed for every two or three animals. The decoys "can act like anything, to fool people." The decoys try to find one another and stay together.

The four girls who made up this game could quickly adjust to accommodate different numbers of players by handing out a few additional animal cards, as long as the last animal was trying to find the first, so that the animals would eventually form a circle. This game was played in silence with no verbal cues; for younger groups, in addition to acting out the animal, they could make animal sounds.

Beat the Clock

Two equal teams are formed on opposite sides of a volleyball net. A player on one team throws a volleyball over the net, and a player on the other team catches it and throws it back. If someone catches the ball for a second time, he must pass it to a person on his side of the net who has not yet handled the ball. Once everyone on both teams has thrown the ball over the net, the players check to see how long it took, then try to beat their record in the next game. A variation of this game is to have everyone on both sides catch the ball and pass to one of their own teammates. The children who invented this game felt that in order to make it really work, they needed to come up with a way to "have more action"—a challenge that perhaps you can ask your children to resolve.

Miss Your Legs

The children break into groups of five, and the groups form lines 5 to 10 feet (about 2 to 3 meters) apart. The first person in each line hikes a ball under her legs to the next person and then runs to the back of the line. The second person then does the same thing, and so on down the line. One point is counted every time the ball is hiked to and successfully caught by the next person in line. After a specific time, players can add up the collective score and then repeat the procedure to try to improve the first score.

In and Out

In this modified form of dodgeball, the group is divided into two, with one half forming a circle around the other half. The people on the outside of the circle throw a beach ball at those in the center. Two balls are in play. If the ball hits a player below the waist, he switches places with the person who threw it. The game is played until everyone has had a chance to be both inside and outside the circle. The children commented that "no one is really out," and the beach ball "doesn't hurt."

To increase cooperation, the players suggested passing the ball once on the outside of the circle before throwing it to the center. This suggestion was tried immediately and was well received. The game works smoothly with a total group of about 14 or 16.

Gym Hattette

Two teams are made up of six people each—the inventors chose three girls and three boys for each team. Each team is trying to get six points. A point is scored when a baseball hat (puck) is directed into the opponent's goal with a stick or pole. Each team has a goalie, two defensive players, two forwards, and a center; the goals are the length of two gym mats (hanging on the wall); everyone on one team must touch the hat (by receiving a pass with his stick) before a team can score; a person can score only once during a game; the hat must be passed (not carried) over the center line.

Gym Hattette was created by girls who played in a competitive ringette league within their community. Ringette resembles noncontact floor hockey and is played with skates, on ice, with a ring for a puck. Their modified semicooperative game of hattette with an all-touch passing rule was well received by the children once the rules became clear.

Baseball Tennis

Baseball Tennis is similar to regular street baseball in that you have a batter, a pitcher, and some fielders. However, a tennis racket is used as the bat, and a beanbag is used as the ball (to ensure everyone can get a hit). The children first tried playing with a tennis ball, but "it went too far." So they switched to a beanbag, which the children have no problem hitting.

Games for Children 13 and Older

Collective-Score Towel Ball

This game is similar to Collective-Score Blanketball except that team members propel a beach ball over the net using towels. Players work in pairs within their teams. One collective point is scored every time the ball goes over the net and is successfully caught by a pair on the other side. The ball must be passed to a second pair before being volleyed back over the net. This game can also be played in groups of three or four and with towels of different sizes and shapes, chosen by players according to their ability and skill level. The number of pairs per side and the number of balls in play are also flexible.

Scooter Basketball

In this game, similar to traditional crosscourt basketball, each player sits on a small wooden or plastic scooter or dolly (a small mover's dolly on casters) that allows free movement in any direction. The player propels himself by pushing off of the floor with his feet. Dribbling is optional. Every player on the team must touch the ball before attempting to score (all-touch rule). Garbage cans or European handball nets can be used as goals, two balls can be in play at once, and a collective scoring system can be applied.

Partner Scooter Basketball

In this version of Scooter Basketball, one partner is on a scooter and the other is not. The standing partner pushes her teammate around the court on the scooter but cannot touch the ball; the seated partner shoots at the goal or passes the ball to another player. Partners later switch positions. Different scoring options can be introduced to account for ability (e.g., shooting into a large net, through a hanging hula hoop, or into a basketball net), and either traditional or collective scores can be counted.

Scooter Towel Ball

Scooter Towel Ball is similar to Scooter Basketball, with a blanket twist. Each player sits on her own scooter or dolly, and players work in pairs, sharing a single towel to carry, pass, catch, and shoot a beach ball at the goal. This game can be played using a traditional scoring procedure with a large goal, no goalie, and an all-touch rule.

Basket-Football

This modified basketball game is played with an American football. There is generally no dribbling. The football is passed to every team member underhand before a shot is attempted into the net. Two points are scored for the ball going through the hoop and one point for just hitting the backboard. The game begins with teams lining up facing each other, and one team hikes the ball. No body contact is allowed.

Other teenagers' ideas include the following:

- For Collective-Score Volleyball games, put blankets or sheets over the net so the receiving team cannot see exactly when the ball is coming over.
- For all-touch games, team members should establish a signal to indicate that a player has not yet received the ball.
- Play table tennis with five people rotating around a big table to see how many times in a row players can get the ball over the net.
- Play some of these games outside in deep snow or in sand.
- Play volleyball with lots of balls in play, using the full length of the gym, with all those who want to play playing at the same time. Try to get balls to go from one end of the gym to the other by passing along the length of the gym before tapping them over the net. Let the kids work out the rules.

EVALUATING AND IMPROVING COOPERATIVE GAMES

When we evaluate our games, we attempt to determine whether the children like the game and whether the game meets the basic objectives of cooperation, acceptance, inclusion, and fun. The main methods for assessing the success of cooperative games are observing, asking questions, and reflecting.

Observing

You can learn a lot by carefully watching children play and by listening closely to their informal comments and not-so-idle chatter. Focused observations over an extended period of time can provide some very valuable information. When I am leading cooperative games sessions with children or adults, I am constantly "reading" the room for how the game is going, how the players are responding, and whether the game is working with respect to the overall objectives of cooperative games.

Basically, I want to see that all the kids seem to be cooperating and having fun. But you can ask yourself more specific questions according to your situation. For example, if I am observing children playing a game I have just introduced, some questions I keep in mind include the following:

- Do the children understand how the game is supposed to be played?
- Is the challenge appropriate for this group of children—is it too difficult, too easy, or just right?
- Is the pace of the game moving well?
- Is everyone focused and "into" the game?
- Is everyone involved in the action?
- Are the kids cooperating, helping, and sharing?
- Are they being considerate of others?
- Are they having fun?
- Do they look as if they feel fully accepted?

One important opportunity that is often overlooked in evaluating many of our games and other educational programs is firsthand experience by the leader, teacher, or assessor. If you want to know what's happening under the Big Turtle shell, what better way than to get under there? You not only hear what's going on but also see it and feel it. You become part of the action! Besides, it's the best chance to learn something from the masters of playful play, the littlest children. Gaining this inside perspective is one of the reasons I so often participate in the games with the children. The other reason is that I have lots of fun playing with them, and it creates a special bond between us. It makes me feel like a kid again, and I like that feeling.

A lot of important feedback can be gleaned from being a keen observer and focused listener during and after the games, in a variety of settings (in the gym, on the field, at the picnic, in the car or bus, in the dressing room, in the hallway, on the way back to the classroom after a gym class, at recess, in the classroom). Parents and siblings of children involved in cooperative games and other positive living skills activities can also provide some very interesting and valuable comments from an outside perspective. What do the children say about the games or activities when they go home? Do they teach any of the activities to their parents, family members, or friends outside of school?

Asking Questions

One of the best ways to get children's feedback on the games they play is simply to ask! After we have played cooperative games, I always gather the group of children close together, with all of us sitting on the floor or ground. I point out some good things I observed—such as how well they played together—and ask them to share highlights of our time together and other thoughts they may have. I also pay attention to how the children respond when I ask them if they want to play a particular game or listen to a particular relaxation activity again. After I have played a number of cooperative games with the children, I often ask what games they want to play today or what audio CDs they want to listen to. The excitement and volume of their responses give you a pretty good idea of what they like best.

Some of the questions I ask children in these group sessions include the following:

- Did you like the game?
- Was the game fun?

Asking is one of the best ways to find out whether children enjoy a game.

- When you were playing the game, did you feel accepted?
- Did you feel included?
- Were you cooperating with others?
- Were others cooperating with you?
- What parts of the game did you like best?
- Is there anything you didn't like about the game?
- Is there anything you think might make the game better or more fun?

When new cooperative rules are introduced (e.g., all touch), here are some questions you might ask:

- What did you think of the new rules? Did you like them?
- How much fun was it to play using these new rules compared with regular rules?
- What was the best thing about the new rules?
- Is there anything you did not like about them?
- Would you make any changes in the new rules to make the game better or more fun?
- Do you think you would want to play using these rules again?

When new cooperative games are introduced, you can ask the children some of the following questions to assess their opinions of the game:

- What did you think of the game? Did you like it?
- Who won? Did you win or lose?
- Did you help in reaching the goal of the game? If yes, how?
- What did you like best about the game?
- Is there anything you did not like?
- Do you have any ideas on how to make the game better or more fun?
- Would you like to play it again?

When children are very familiar with a cooperative games program (e.g., after 8 weeks of playing cooperative games), these questions might be more appropriate:

- How do you feel about the games we have been playing? Do you like them?
- What do you like best about the games?
- Is there anything you do not like?

- Do you feel happy or sad when playing these games?
- Which games do you like best? Why?
- Which games do you like least? Why?
- Do you feel that you are helping one another in these games?
- Do you ever feel left out or excluded in these games?
- Do you ever feel that you lost in the new games? If yes, when? If no, why not?
- Do you ever feel that you lose in regular games? If yes, when? If no, why not?
- Can you think of any ways to make these new games better?
- Can you think of any ways to make regular games better?
- If you could play any kinds of games you wanted in your gym class (or at a picnic, play days, and the like), what kinds of games would you play?
- Would you have any special rules?

The only precautionary note when asking a group of children a question such as "How did you like that game?" is to ensure that different types of children get a chance to respond. At certain age levels, if the group is competitive and only a couple of the most aggressive or assertive kids get to respond, their opinions will not likely be representative of the feelings of the rest of the children. The goal in these group meetings is to get a feel for the whole group and to also give those who are not normally highly vocal in a group context a chance to express their views. Often I go around the group asking each child, or different children in the group, to comment on how she felt about the game. "Jewelia, how did you feel when you were doing the Spaghetti Toes game?" "John, did you like the balloon and hoops game?" "Dani, how did you feel about that game?"

Another assessment option is to approach children individually in order to seek out their personal feelings and suggestions for improving games or activities. You can do this by talking briefly to individual children on a person-to-person basis. Other options include asking children to draw pictures of their favorite cooperative games, or with a class of older children (who can write), asking them to respond to a brief questionnaire about the games they played or CDs they listened to. Whenever adults show a genuine interest in children's opinions and act on their input, it is a novel experience for at least some of the kids. It feels good to be respected and to know that others value your opinions, especially as a child.

With young children, an excellent way to quickly assess how they feel about the games is to use pictures, ranging from smiling faces to

(a) Ask preschool and kindergarten children how they feel while playing a game. *(b)* Using a more developed scale, ask older children to rate how they feel while playing.

sad faces. Immediately after a game is over, the players simply make a mark under the face with the expression closest to their feelings. With kindergarten children, we use three faces (happy, in between, sad); with some developmentally challenged groups, we use just two faces (happy, sad); older groups respond to a range of five faces.

Reflecting

After a cooperative games session, I reflect on what went well and what could be improved for this particular group of children. If a game did not go as well as I had hoped, I think about where it might have broken down—was it related to the structure of the game, my communication with the children, the age level, or a lack of action? Or was the game simply not appropriate for this group of children? My reflections are often enhanced or more accurate when I ask children for their constructive feedback right after they have played some games with me. They like to be consulted and given an opportunity to express their views. It makes them feel valued and respected, and I really do value and respect their opinions. I like to act on their positive thoughts and cooperative ideas, to give them a try, the sooner the better.

ADDRESSING PROBLEMS

If I see that a game is too slow, or there is not enough action, or the children have not yet figured out how to do the skills together, I will observe for a little while before stepping in because the problem often resolves itself. If it does not resolve itself, I will step in and make adjustments right there on the spot if I believe it will improve the flow, respectfulness, or joyfulness of that game or the next game.

If I observe a child behaving in a way that is disrespectful or hurtful to another child (e.g., leaving a child out, pushing or hitting another child, or hogging the balloon or ball that they are supposed to be sharing), I immediately walk over to that child and use it as a teachable moment. I usually bend down or kneel down to the child's level, ask him to look at my eyes, and then quietly explain how we want to play this game. I will often then direct the child's attention to a pair or group of children that is playing the game well and challenge him to try to play the game that way.

If a number of children are not respecting the rules of cooperative games (which has been rare in my experience), I use a tambourine to get their attention to stop the game, then address the issue with the whole group. In this case, I comment on the positives and then respectfully point out specifically how I feel the group can improve the game for everyone. I often involve the children in the discussion to see what they think should be done. Then I immediately try to implement any of their positive suggestions so they know this is not just an exercise . . . I really do want their ideas! I want their input to make the games as fun as they can be for all the players. I also know that if I listen to the children and act on their good ideas, they will feel important and valued and will be much more likely to continue to contribute their input when I ask for it.

8 A New Beginning: Turning Ideas Into Positive Action

For most of my life, I have worked with high-level performers pursuing personal excellence in many different domains; at the same time, I have worked closely with children to teach them skills for cooperation and positive living to enhance the overall quality of their lives. Some people have asked me, "How can you work with high-level performers on pursuing excellence and at the same time work with children on cooperation and positive interaction? Isn't there a conflict there?" I have never experienced a conflict in pursuing these two important paths at the same time.

Excellence is extremely important in our world—in parenting, teaching, working, consulting, and performing in every human endeavor—and becoming excellent is largely a cooperative venture. You can't do it totally on your own. Cooperation and collaboration play a big part in nurturing successful relationships and enhancing performance in all areas of life.

As a society, we have gone overboard on competition and inadequately addressed the vital role of empathy and cooperation. My cooperative work with children and teenagers is designed to help them excel at living and teach them the true value of respect and cooperation. And if they choose to compete, it gives them the tools to pursue their goals in a constructive way, with less stress and a healthier perspective. Genuine cooperation helps people become better performers, better partners, better teammates, and better people.

My experience has shown me that destructive competition can destroy people, relationships, teams, and organizations. If children learn to excel at cooperation and bring a healthy perspective to their performance pursuits and their lives, it will free them to be better people, better teammates, and less-stressed performers. What most people are lacking at this point in our evolution is a sense of balance and joy in their pursuits and their lives, which is important for all people in all pursuits. My work with children is an attempt to fill this void. This is my quest.

When we witness the extent and depth of human destructiveness in so many corners of the world, we sometimes forget that there were and still are many societies, and people of all ages on our planet, who are cooperative and caring. A basic human right for all people, of all ages, in all countries should be freedom from abuse and violence. When visiting some of the world's most peaceful and cooperative cultures, one thing that really struck me was the extent to which their children's play and games are cooperative and inclusive. Almost all their games are cooperative in nature, and if a game is competitive in structure, it is still played in a cooperative and respectful way. Children are not divided into winners and losers though their games. Children are not excluded by other children in their play. Play is a special place for coming together in positive and joyful ways.

This high level of cooperation and respectful inclusion that I witnessed in children at very early ages in cooperative cultures stands in stark contrast to what has become common, or "normal," in more abusive or abrasive cultures in the world. In less-cooperative and more-destructive societies, children's early play and game experiences are competitive, restrictive, and sometimes abusive. Even in free play (e.g., in the streets or in school yards), many children are excluded or directly confronted and told by other children, "You can't play with us!" even at 4 or 5 or 6 years of age. Being rejected in this way can be very harmful and hurtful for young children who are just beginning to develop a sense of their own value among their peers. Those children who are the perpetrators of this abuse and rejection in play are also negatively affected. They learn that bullying or hurting others physically or psychologically is OK or even good. If we follow this path to its logical conclusion, we end up with a culture of insensitive, nonempathetic, uncaring children who turn into adults who have honed these abusive traits to perfection, therein providing little or no hope for harmony within their lives, their relationships, or our world.

In every culture, we begin with beautiful little babies who have the capacity to be anything or do anything. There is not a destructive fiber in their being. They are pure at the start. Therein lies our hope for the future. Children live what they learn, and it is initially through play and games that children learn most about their world and how they should be in their world. Every child plays, and all children are greatly influenced by how they play and what they learn through their play. Play is their early window to the world. It is essential that we work together in all corners of the world to make these early childhood play experiences as positive, inclusive, and life enhancing as possible. If we successfully create positive foundations for caring and sharing early in a child's life, through play and games and any other mediums available to us, we all gain something of immense value.

Our need for positive experiences in children's play, games, and lives is clear, and the opportunities we have to fulfill these needs are exciting. Somewhere we've gotten off track, and I've tried in this book to suggest some ways to get back on a more positive course. On behalf of children, I am asking you to act on some of these suggestions and to go further by creating better or more compassionate ways of playing and living. No one book or person can provide all the answers. We need a cooperative effort to move forward in meaningful ways. I encourage you to act by moving forward in your own positive direction from the humble beginnings I offer here. Think of the big picture. How do you want your children and our world to be? Then be as open, flexible, and imaginative as possible in creating opportunities that will take us along this path . . . one little step at a time. See page 156 for a few guidelines for playing joyfully.

Sometimes we have to look back to look forward. Sometimes we need to look beyond our own experience or outside our own culture to find meaningful direction. Sometimes we need to look inward and trust our own intuition to find meaning and inspiration. When I look down this path, the vision that often surfaces is more playful play, more gentle games, more games of sharing and caring, and more joyful lives.

If we put our minds together and focus on what is best for children and their play, we certainly have the capacity to help all children become the good and productive people they all have the potential to be. By increasing children's joyful interactions, by nurturing their great capacity for human empathy, and by reducing the stress in their lives, we will take a giant leap forward on this planet. We can start to do this today. You and I can take the first step right now. Together, we can help the children in our lives, and those who follow, to inherit a healthier and more compassionate world in which to live, love, work, and play.

As we move along this positive path with heart, try to share your ideas and successful experiences so that more children, parents, and teachers can benefit from them. If you create new cooperative games or find an approach or activity or positive medium for change that works well, share your creations with others. Further, send me an e-mail. I'd love to hear about your experiences and will make every effort to share the wealth of ideas that flow from your collective wisdom. This way we will all be winners.

I wish you success in embracing the simple joys of each day; in nurturing the best in yourself; and in being a positive force for each child with whom you live, work, or play.

Embrace the simple joys,

Terry Orlick (e-mail: excel@zoneofexcellence.com)

POSITIVE GUIDELINES FOR PLAYING JOYFULLY

Reminders for Teachers, Parents, or Leaders

Nurture fun and cooperation.

Maximize play time for each child.

Remind children that they are responsible for keeping the game fun and safe for everyone.

If a problem arises during play or games, stop the game. Engage the children in a brief discussion on how to solve the problem and why it is important to do so. Use problems or conflicts as teachable moments—lessons for being better next time.

Ask the children for their ideas, and integrate their suggestions in the games and activities wherever possible.

Encourage children to make up fun rules, fun games, and fun names for their games and teams.

Adjust the rules to keep the games playful, cooperative, respectful, active, inclusive, fun, and safe.

Watch the children having fun, and let a little of their enthusiasm and pure joy rub off onto you.

Join in the play with them whenever you can.

Find something to be positive about in each child with whom you interact each day.

The path to teaching children to live with harmony and a generous heart is achieved step by step. Take one little step forward each day.

Stay positive with yourself, and embrace the simple joys in your own life.

Reminders for Children

Everyone plays.

Everyone has fun.

Everyone cooperates.

Everyone is accepted.

Everyone is included.

No one is left out.

Everyone is nice on everyone's feelings.

Reminders to Put up on the Wall

In addition to happy pictures or children's drawings of kids playing together joyfully and cooperatively, the following messages can be placed around the room:

Everyone has more fun when we cooperate.

Everyone likes to feel included and accepted.

Everyone likes to be treated with respect.

Everyone has a right to be respected.

Find some happy highlights every day.

Appendix

COOPERATIVE PLAY DAYS

During cooperative play days, children from all age levels (and adults, too) are integrated on a single team. They can play cooperative games you select, teach one another the cooperative games they know, and all have a good time playing together. They can even create new cooperative games. It's a great way to bring children of various ages and families together, to allow them to get to know one another better, to teach others, to learn from one another, to be responsible for one another, and to help one another reach mutually beneficial goals. We have had many successful cooperative play days both in and out of school settings.

I would like to share with you one cooperative games day, which was spearheaded by Sally Olsen, a special-education teacher and mother of three. Sally was the inspiration behind one of the world's first bilingual cooperative games family play days. I asked her to recap the day in writing so that others could gain from her experience. What follows is her response to my request.

> What a day! When we woke up, the fog was so thick you couldn't see the end of the driveway. When we arrived at a local park, it might as well have been raining, the dew was so heavy. But we set up, ever optimists, and at the appointed time people started coming—and they kept coming. We spread out the parachute, which promptly got soaked on the grass, and the people congregated around it to start the parachute game.
>
> We were cold and damp, but soon the exercise and warm feelings of cooperating with others to have fun won out over the cold day. We played most of the 14 games we had chosen and invented 3 more—all with a spirit of cooperation. We had a great time.
>
> The organizing committee of three chose 14 of the games in this book to play:
>
> Cooperative Musical Chairs
> Barnyard
> Toesie Roll
> Sticky Popcorn
> Cooperative Musical Hugs
> Bump and Scoot
> Human Tangles
> Log Roll
> Collective Orbit
> Balloon Keep-Up

Parachute
Tiptoe Through the Tulips
Shoe Twister
Grasshopper in the Blanket

We chose these games because we are a nursery school organization, and we knew we would have a lot of preschoolers present. We also chose games that used as little equipment as possible. Except for the two successful and unusual props—the parachute and a 10-foot weather balloon—we used some small beach balls and improvised the rest with the people present. When we didn't have chairs for Cooperative Musical Chairs, we used people with strong backs who knelt, side by side, on all fours. We eliminated a chair when the music stopped and the "chair" then got up to join the people skipping around. When we didn't have a net for Bump and Scoot, we got five people to join hands and be the net in the middle of the field. The "net" was allowed to hit the ball with their heads, knees, or anything else they could manage without letting go of hands. They also moved from side to side on the field, which added some interest to the game.

In reflecting back on the day, we believe the following ideas might be useful to anyone organizing a similar play day.

Write the instructions out on a large board or pad. Here is an example:

TOESIE ROLL

Maximum number in one group: an even number (10, 32). Kindergarten children giggle all the way through this game. Some older people have also been known to let out a chuckle or two. Partners simply lie stretched out on the grass, feet to feet, and attempt to roll across the grass, keeping their toes touching throughout. Variations: Try it with only the toes of the right feet connected, with legs crisscrossed. Try the whole thing with bare feet—we dare you!

We printed the games in French and English and drew a red border around the games that were most suited to preschoolers. We stapled the posters on sharpened poles or stakes with wooden crosspieces. We suggest that you put out only four posters at the beginning of the day (for groups totaling 80 to 100). Cooperative Musical Chairs, Human Tangles, Barnyard, and Parachute seemed to get people going. When people looked around for something new, we put up another poster. It was heartwarming to see games start up spontaneously throughout the day. Every once in a while, a Sticky Popcorn group would erupt and spread over the field, gathering up everyone in their popping. The log rollers decided to finish their games by all rolling over the edge of a gently sloped hill. We found that the parachute and the weather balloon were excellent in starting people off at the beginning of the day when the group was small and again after lunch when they tended to sit and ruminate too long.

You can buy a parachute from a school supplies games equipment store or your local skydiving club. The weather balloons are found in surplus stores or through advertisements in magazines such as *Popular Science.* You don't need helium to blow up the balloons. Put the hose of your vacuum cleaner on the exhaust so that the hot air blows out and blows up the balloon. It is better to have several balloons because they pop easily. We never blew ours up more than 5 feet (1.5 meters) in diameter.

We all agreed that it is better to have a supervisor at each game—someone who can get a group going but be able to let people take over and adapt or invent new games if they can. You also need an extra supervisor for games such as Cooperative Musical Chairs if you are using people as chairs—someone to make sure no one sits on the chairs' heads or dives onto their backs. For Log Roll, we needed someone to launch the riders in the proper manner and to help the riders off at the end so they wouldn't kneel on the last person. We also found that smaller children don't mix well with bigger ones for the logs. The smaller ones tend to slip down, and the rider might hit their heads with his knees.

We invented three games that day. The following version of Floating Parachute was passed on by a mother who played it in kindergarten with her child's class. You roll up the edge of the parachute (for a good grip) and pull gently until all the material touches the ground when laid flat. Try to get a large person pulling on each rib (the stitching forms the rib) and the smaller children pulling between the ribs. With everyone squatting down, get the parachute as flat on the ground as you can. A small child goes in the middle and lies down. Then everyone starts making waves in the parachute. Gradually make the waves bigger and bigger, and then someone with a loud voice yells, "One, two, three—up!" At this, everyone stands up and pulls the parachute waist high. The child in the middle will float up about 2 feet (just over half a meter). I'm sure the children think it is much higher because the parachute billows in huge mountains of air around them. They will settle down fairly softly, and they love it.

Did we have a good day? Did we enjoy the games? Did we enjoy playing with each other? *Yes,* and we know you will too.

Resources

AUDIO CDS

Positive living skills audio CDs for children and youth by Terry Orlick (all CDs available from www.zoneofexcellence.com or Amazon.com)

Spaghetti Toes: Positive Living Skills for Children (2004).

Changing Channels: Positive Living Skills for Children (2005).

Focusing Through Distractions: Positive Living Skills for Teens and Adults (2005).

Relaxation and Joyful Living: Positive Living Skills for Teens and Adults (2005).

BOOKS

Orlick, T. (1982). *The second cooperative sports and games book.* New York: Random House.

Orlick, T. (1997). *Nice on my feelings: Nurturing the best in children and parents.* Carp, ON: Creative Bound. (www.creativebound.com)

Orlick, T. (1998). *Embracing your potential: Steps to self-discovery, balance, and success in sports, work, and life.* Champaign, IL: Human Kinetics.

Orlick, T. (2000). *In pursuit of excellence: How to win in sport and life through mental training.* Champaign, IL: Human Kinetics.

Orlick, T. (2001). *Feeling great: Teaching children to excel at living* (3rd edition). Carp, ON: Creative Bound. (www.creativebound.com)

Orlick, T. (2002). Enhancing children's sport and life experiences. In F. Smoll & R. Smith (Eds.), *Children and youth in sport.* Dubuque, IA: Kendall/Hunt.

COOPERATIVE TABLE GAMES

Family Pastimes, by Jim Deacove, RR #4, Perth, ON, Canada K7H 3C6. www.familypastimes.com.

ARTICLES

Cox, J., & Orlick, T. (1996). Feeling great: Teaching life skills to children. *Journal of Performance Education* 1, 115-130.

Gilbert, J., & Orlick, T. (2002).Teaching skills for stress control and positive thinking to elementary school children. *Journal of Excellence* 7, 54-66. (Note: *Journal of Excellence* is a free online journal available at www.zoneofexcellence.com.)

Gilbert, M., & Orlick, T. (1996). Evaluation of a life skills program with grade two children. *Elementary School Guidance and Counseling Journal* 31, 139-151.

Hester, K., & Orlick, T. (2005). The effects of a positive living skills program on ADHD children. *Journal of Excellence* 10, 25-41. (www.zoneofexcellence.com)

Klingenberg, M., & Orlick, T. (2002). Teaching positive living skills to a family with special needs. *Journal of Excellence* 7, 5-35. (www.zoneofexcellence.com)

Koudys, J., & Orlick, T. (2002). Coping with cancer: Lessons from a pediatric cancer patient and his family. *Journal of Excellence* 7, 36-53. (www.zoneofex cellence.com)

Mender, J., Kerr, R., & Orlick, T. (1982). A cooperative games program for learning disabled children. *International Journal of Sport Psychology* 13(4), 222-233.

Orlick, T. (1972). A socio-psychological analysis of early sports participation. (Doctoral dissertation). Edmonton: University of Alberta.

Orlick, T. (1974). The athletic drop-out: A high price for inefficiency. *CAHPER Journal* 41(2), 21-27.

Orlick, T. (1974). Sports participation: A process of shaping behaviour. *Human Factors* 16(5), 558-561.

Orlick, T. (1977). Cooperative games. *JOPHER Journal: Special Issue on Children* 48(7), 33-35.

Orlick, T. (1977). Traditional Inuit games: Looking back to look forward. *CAHPER Journal* 43(5), 6-10.

Orlick, T. (1979). Children's games: Following the path that has heart. *Elementary School Guidance and Counseling Journal* 14(2), 156-161.

Orlick, T. (1979). Cooperative games: Cooperative lives. *Recreation Research Review* 6(4), 9-12.

Orlick, T. (1980). *Tumbuna pilai: Traditional Siwai games.* (Research Rep. No. 5). Papua New Guinea: University of Papua New Guinea, Education Research Unit, and North Solomons Provincial Government.

Orlick, T. (1981). Cooperative play socialization among preschool children. *Journal of Individual Psychology* 2(1), 54-64.

Orlick, T. (1981). Positive socialization via cooperative games. *Developmental Psychology* 17(4), 426-429.

Orlick, T. (1983). Enhancing love and life mostly through play and games. *Journal of Humanistic Education and Development* 21(4), 153-164.

Orlick, T. (2002). Nurturing positive living skills for children: Feeding the heart and soul of humanity. *Journal of Excellence* 7, 86-98. (www.zoneofexcellence.com)

Orlick, T., Zhou, Q.Y., & Partington, J. (1990). Cooperation and conflict among Chinese and Canadian kindergarten children. *Canadian Journal of Behavioural Science* 22(1), 20-25.

St-Denis, M., & Orlick, T. (1996). Positive perspectives intervention with fourth grade children. *Elementary School Guidance and Counseling Journal* 31, 52-63.

Taylor, S., & Orlick, T. (2004). An analysis of a children's relaxation/stress control skills program in an alternative elementary school. *Journal of Excellence* 9, 89-109. (www.zoneofexcellence.com)

About the Author

Terry Orlick, PhD, is a professor in the school of human kinetics at the University of Ottawa in Ottawa, Ontario, Canada. He has worked with children in creative ways for more than 30 years as a teacher, coach, researcher, and parent, and he has written hundreds of articles and several books dedicated to enhancing the lives of children and parents. He created the unique Positive Living Skills Program (PLS), which teaches children skills for positive interaction, focusing, relaxation, stress control, and positive thinking.

Orlick has also served as president of the International Society for Mental Training and Excellence and received the Honor Award for Excellence in Teaching from the University of Ottawa. In 2001 he was honored by the International Society of Sport Psychology for his significant contributions to national and international sport psychology through leadership, research, and community service.